Strategies, Leadership and Complexity in Crisis and Emergency Operations

T0383966

Stig O. Johannessen has produced a masterpiece that combines
and solid empirical details; it is a timely must-read for everyor
plexity, strategy and leadership in crisis and emergency operatic

—Dr. Zhichang Zhu, South-China Normal University, China,
Author (with Ikujiro Nonaka) of *Pragmatic Strategy:
Eastern Wisdom, Global Success*

This book is a must-read for anyone with an interest in strategy. It combines highly readable accounts of two major internationally significant events with state-of-the art analysis and theorising. In taking us well beyond the somewhat tired debates of mainstream strategy, it convincingly suggests new possibilities and ways of engaging in the complex and paradoxical landscapes of strategy in modern organizations. It turns compelling accounts of real-life events into valuable lessons for scholarly practitioners and practically minded scholars alike. Again, a must-read.

—**Professor Donald MacLean**, Adam Smith Business School,
University of Glasgow, Scotland

A compelling study of cases where organizations are pushed way beyond what they were prepared or designed for. Stig O. Johannessen not only notes the brittleness of hierarchy and bureaucracy, but helps us identify sources of organizational resilience, innovation and hope.

—**Professor Sidney Dekker**, Director, Safety Science Innovation Lab,
Griffith University, Australia

This book gives brand new insights into what made the police and the military react as they did in two famous cases of terrorism and international political crises. The explanations given using the complexity approach of the book provide a thought provoking contribution to analysis of emergency and crises response.

—**Professor Ira Helsloot**, Radboud Universiteit Nijmegen, Netherlands

Strategies, Leadership and Complexity in Crisis and Emergency Operations brings together the themes of strategy, operational leadership, and organizational dynamics in the context of crisis and emergency operations. The result is a book that is timely and relevant for research and leadership in the police, the military, and other organizations involved in operations in highly dynamic and critical contexts.

The book is based on research material from two major events of international crisis and national emergency in 2011: the police operation in response to the terrorist attacks in Norway that left 77 people killed and hundreds injured, and the military response to the Libyan crisis during the Arab Spring. The author discusses and compares the dynamics within the Norwegian police and military during the crisis and emergency operations.

The book draws on theories of complexity, organizational communication, and social psychology to create a vivid inquiry of the case material and to develop a fresh understanding of the ambiguous landscapes of practices of communication, power, identity, and ethics that transform hierarchies, strategies, decision-making, and sensemaking processes in stressful situations during crises and emergencies.

Stig O. Johannessen is Professor of Organization and Leadership at Nord University, Norway.

Routledge Advances in Management and Business Studies

For a full list of titles in this series, please visit www.routledge.com/series/SE0305

Strategies, Leadership and Complexity in Crisis and Emergency Operations

Stig O. Johannessen

Routledge
Taylor & Francis Group

LONDON AND NEW YORK

First published 2018 by Routledge

2 Park Square, Milton Park, Abingdon, Oxforshire OX14 4RN

52 Vanderbilt Avenue, New York, NY 10017

Routledge is an imprint of the Taylor & Francis Group, an informa business

First issued in paperback 2019

Library of Congress Cataloging-in-Publication Data
Names: Johannessen, Stig O., author.
Title: Strategies, leadership and complexity in crisis and emergency operations / by Stig O Johannessen.
Description: New York : Routledge, [2017] | Includes index.
Identifiers: LCCN 2017015354 | ISBN 9781138889224 (hardback) | ISBN 9781315713038 (ebook)
Subjects: LCSH: Crisis management. | Communication in crisis management. | Leadership. | Strategic planning.
Classification: LCC HD49 .J65 2017 | DDC 658.4/092—dc23
LC record available at https://lccn.loc.gov/2017015354

ISBN: 978-1-138-88922-4 (hbk)
ISBN: 978-0-367-24279-4 (pbk)

Typeset in Sabon
by Apex CoVantage, LLC

This book is dedicated to my long-term collaborator, working partner, and friend Dr Bjørner Bodøgaard Christensen, in appreciation of our conversations and common efforts.

Contents

Acknowledgements

It would not have been possible to write and publish this book without the influence, support, and help of many outstanding people. I want to thank all who have spent time collaborating with me over the years and have thus been a long-lived source of inspiration to my way of thinking about groups, organizations, and leadership practices. Especially, I want to mention Ralph D. Stacey, Farhad Dalal, and Nol Groot, whose influence is more ingrained in this book than the cited references might indicate.

The cases examined in this book have come about as the result of interviews and conversations with many people over a long period. I want to extend my sincerest thanks to all who have shared so many of their experiences from the Norwegian police and the Royal Norwegian Air Force. I especially want to thank Major General Inge Kampenes for his continued support and interest in exploring complexity in organizational and leadership practices in the military.

My thanks go also to the anonymous reviewers, to my colleagues, and to professionals, all of whom were kind enough to give me critical and encouraging comments on different parts and details of the manuscript at different stages.

I wish to thank the sponsors of the research. The Fritt Ord Foundation, Norway, sponsored the data collection for the 22 July case, and The Royal Norwegian Air Force sponsored the data collection for the Libyan case. Nord University, Bodø, Norway, provided me the time and space to write the book.

I want to express my great appreciation of David Varley and his team at Routledge for their encouraging, professional, and patient guidance, and equally to Catriona Turner for her crucial help in advising on English language issues and for language checking at various stages.

Finally, and most important of all, my deepest gratitude go to my fabulous family May, Bendik, Magnus, and Jakob. My work would not have been possible without their continued support and understanding.

Trondheim, Norway
March 2017
Stig Ole Johannessen

1 Introduction

The purpose of this study is to describe and interpret the organizational complexity and dynamics in two cases of crisis and emergency operations with a particular view towards how strategies and leadership emerge in situations that are out of the ordinary. The study has sprung from two basic questions: Why did the police react *slower* than expected to a national terror emergency? Why did the military react *faster* than expected to an international political crisis?

Although these questions have motivated a comparison of two very different situations of crisis and emergency, the starting point for both cases, and for the organizations involved, was that the events were extraordinary and dramatic, and outside any scenario most people had imagined or for which the organizations had prepared. Clearly, there had to be many differences as well as similarities in the details of the organizational responses, but on the surface, the issue of *time* stands out as a profound difference between them. This issue also turned out to be the most important differentiator in the public response. Generally speaking, the military effort was hailed as impressive and heroic, and a sign of a high degree of professionalism, while the police effort was subjected to a public inquiry, during which it was condemned as having failed to protect the public against terrorism. In the wake of this public purging, a politically motivated reform emerged to reorganize the entire Norwegian police (Johannessen, 2015). However, no research in the aftermath of the events has attempted to explore the above questions with the aim of understanding the organizational complexity underlying the response times in the two cases.

In this study, the seemingly simple questions of time have necessitated an in-depth examination of the details of the events in order to bring to the forefront the *dynamics of organizational breakdown* and the simultaneous *transformation* of formal hierarchical organization into informal network organization during crisis and emergency. In the highly volatile contexts of the events, the meaning of strategy and leadership also transformed, from static formalities of hierarchical levels to a dynamic interaction in which *communication*, *power*, *identity*, and *ethics* drove, defined, and, above all, differentiated group and organizational practices between different hierarchies, and at the different formal levels of hierarchies.

Although often experienced, the collapse of hierarchical organization and the spontaneous emergence of network organizing in crisis and emergency operations is poorly understood. This raises the general question: why, in the heat of the moment, do some organizations that are responding to crises immediately manage to redefine any pretext they have of authority, organization, and coordination (i.e. strategies and leadership), while others do not? This is a challenge for organizational actors and leaders involved in crisis and emergency operations, but also one for organizational research. The present study aspires to contribute in the search for more knowledge to answer this question.

The study is shaped within a broad field of organizational process research, and in particular, it explores dynamical phenomena of organization and leadership from a complexity theoretical understanding of organizations. As this approach deals specifically with interactions, dynamics, unpredictability, self-organizing structuring of order, and sudden structural breakdown, it seems to be well suited for studies of crisis and emergency operations.

Crisis and Emergency Operations

Research on organizational issues in crisis management and crisis response has been conducted in response to a variety of events throughout history (Rosenthal, Boin & Comfort, 2001; Helslott et al., 2012), from the Mann Gulch fire in 1949, an event that was geographically and historically remote from public scrutiny and academic analysis until light was shed on it much later (Maclean, 1992; Weick, 1993), to more recent spectacular and hugely public events that have undergone intense scrutiny and academic analysis with wide consequences, such as the 1986 space shuttle Challenger accident (Rogers, 1986), the 11 September 2001 terrorist attacks in the USA (The National Commission on Terrorist Attacks Upon the United States, 2004; Pfeifer, 2007), the 2005 Hurricane Katrina in the USA (Schneider, 2005; Farazmand, 2009; Boin et al., 2010), and the 2011 earthquake and tsunami followed by a nuclear disaster in Fukushima, Japan (The National Diet of Japan, 2012; Kadota, Varnam & Tokuhiro, 2014; Casto, 2014). These events are not characterized primarily by the scale of their destruction and number of deaths – the death toll range from the seven astronauts on Challenger to an estimated 15,000 people in Japan – but rather all events were *national traumas* that caused a nationwide collective, organizational, institutional, and political state of shock.

This was also the case for one of the studies in this book, the terrorist attacks in Oslo and on Utøya in 2011. For Norway, they fall into the same stream of dramatic national emergency and trauma as the above-mentioned events were for their respective countries.

The second case study falls into a different category, that of international military operations. However, this operation too was a response to a national trauma in Libya, where a brutal civil war was breaking out in the early days of the 'Arab Spring' uprisings in North Africa in 2011. The case shows the organizational mobilizing response of the Royal Norwegian Air Force as a small part of a much larger and massive rally of mainly NATO military forces in the Mediterranean. The military forces were sent to Libya in response to a UN Security Council resolution to protect civilians from being massacred by Muammar Gaddafi's forces as part of the crackdown on the rebel forces.

In both cases, and as for other national trauma events, organizational and decision-making processes were later subjected to public inquiries (NOU, 2012; House of Commons Foreign Affairs Committee, 2016a, 2016b). However, to date, there has not been any systematic research into the issues of the dynamics of strategies, leadership, and organizational complexity in the events, or any attempts to draw specific and general knowledge from comparisons between the two events, hence the purpose of this book.

In contrast to routine emergencies such as those handled by fire departments, hospitals, and police on a daily basis, crises are associated with serious threats to society, life, health, and property, which demand urgent responses in uncertain contexts (Boin et al., 2005). Clearly, there are a great variety of issues and research problems coming out of the immense complexity of large dramatic events, including the responses from a variety of professional organizations. There are issues *before and after* a crisis, such as public management, policies, strategies, systems, and practices for operational training and preparations, as well as issues to do with inquiries, politics, reforms, learning, and organizational change. *During* a crisis there will be problems related to leadership and decision-making, crisis communication, and phenomena related to stress and performance in very dangerous situations for the responding individuals, groups, and organizations. Additionally, there are various differentiations, definitions, concepts, and theories, which can be used to approach such a multitude of issues and problems.

Following an extensive literature review, Casto (2014) distinguishes *extreme events*, *extreme contexts*, and *routine crises*. In line with Hannah et al. (2009) he suggests that extreme events must be separated from routine crises since they are of an intolerable magnitude to the organization in contrast to just being a threat to organizational goals. Furthermore, extreme events are distinguished from routine crises by the ambiguity of cause and effect and the means of resolution in combination with low probability. In this sense, the terrorist attacks on 22 July 2011 in Norway clearly were extreme events for the police. However, whether the call for immediate action from the Air Force to enforce a no-fly zone over Libya together with allies was an extreme event for the Air Force is open for discussion.

Moreover, extreme events have a non-characteristic preparation time in the sense that organizations involved in the events are not fully prepared. They may have long preparation time, but will be unprepared for the specific event. This was the situation in the 22 July case. As far as the Norwegian military was concerned, they had long prepared for similar events as the Libya situation, but not specifically for Libya. The crisis ended up being handled both as routine and as a response to an extreme event, the latter specifically concerning the initial attacks on civilians in Benghazi by Gaddafi's forces. The Libya event, therefore, does not fall neatly into one category but raises interesting questions about *emergent strategic response*, which are investigated more closely in the case study.

Extreme events can combine with other events or follow closely after one another to form an *extreme context* of high complexity. One example is the March 2011 context in Japan, in which there was a domino effect of earthquake, tsunami, and nuclear power plant meltdown at Fukushima, subsequently followed by additional social disaster for thousands of people (Casto, 2014). Other examples of extreme contexts are Hurricane Katrina, 9/11, not forgetting the vast extreme context and total collapse of societies and states catalyzed partly by the Western military response to the 9/11 attacks, in the region of Afghanistan, Iraq, Syria, and Libya.

The terrorist bomb in Oslo in 2011 was in itself an extreme event, but when it was followed a couple of hours later by a mass shooting 38 kilometres from Oslo, the situation turned into an extreme context, primarily for the police, but also for other emergency responders. Despite the serious nature of the bombing of government buildings, the massacre of young people by shooting arguably transformed the event into the combination of an extreme context and a national trauma. The military mobilization from a coalition of members and non-members of NATO to enforce a UN decision that sanctioned military action on a member country that was rapidly decaying into civil war was clearly a response to intervene in an extreme context and potentially deal with it. In this sense, both operations analyzed in the case studies share the characteristics of being organizational responses to national traumatic events in extreme contexts.

Nevertheless, I emphasize that the two cases are separated by a time dimension and, for some actors, a great difference in the degree of danger. In order to shed light on this distinction, I have chosen to use the terms crisis and emergency, and not extreme events and extreme contexts. Both cases in the book clearly fall into the category of crisis, but an ongoing terrorist attack is an emergency demanding an extremely quick police response.

Although the situation was explosive and the demand for military intervention came sooner than most had expected, the Libya situation emerged over several days, then weeks and ultimately months compared with the minutes to three hours in the police operation on 22 July. The Libya situation was an international political crisis, during which politicians called for swift international military action, but unlike the terrorist attacks in Norway, it was not an emergency. However, I will return to the question of whether the politicians and military confused the crisis with an emergency by overreacting as if the military was a sort of international police force.

Boin et al. (2005) suggest that crisis studies can be separated into those looking at the level of strategic leadership and those researching the operational level of the people directly involved in the crisis. This book crosses these and other abstract levels of organization, and demonstrates what happens when organizations are seen as dynamical interactions and emerging organizational practices performed by people during crises and emergencies.

Theoretical Approach

The theory base of this study is drawn from general complexity theories in organizational studies (Johannessen & Kuhn, 2012). For the purpose of generating a more precise contextualized theorizing on crisis and emergency operations, the view of complexity is energized with a number of theoretical insights integrated into the discussions and referred to throughout the book, some of which concern ideas of organizations as communication and authority (Taylor & Van Every, 2014); power, ideology and group identity (Dalal, 1998); and group dynamics and behaviour in circumstances of high organizational stress (Weick, 2001). Among the ideas I have found particularly helpful within organizational complexity theory are those of Stacey (2010) and his sources in social theory, namely George Herbert Mead (1934) and Norbert Elias (1939; 1991).

Based on these sources of inspiration, I have developed a complexity theoretical framework for studying organizational practices during crises and emergencies. I propose that organizations responding to crisis and emergencies consist of a number of conflicting organizational practices that are differentiated by the practitioners' understanding of *communication, power, identity*, and *ethics*. The different practices are defined by acts of inclusion and exclusion, and the insider-outsider dynamics constructed by them. Most importantly, the *interactions* between operational, bureaucratic, and political practitioners before, during, and after a crisis are crucially important for how strategy, leadership, and organization are understood and performed *as practice* by different organizational practitioners.

One central idea of this book is to explore how the multiple meanings of strategy and leadership anchored in the different organizational practices deeply influence how organizations respond to crisis and emergencies. A key problem is that of *coordination* in unpredictable and dynamic contexts. To uphold standardized procedures and decision-making at the same time as creative improvisation emerges from many actors who lack certainty and relevant information in local situations inevitably means that coordination and collaboration across local contexts becomes a great challenge. As a theory problem, this is at the core of what complexity theorists have been exploring for many years, particularly in the form of computer model simulations of *complex adaptive systems* (i.e. networks of small units (agents) that interact on the basis of local information or rules) (Kauffmann, 1993; Holland, 1998; Allen, 1998).

In simulations of complex adaptive systems, the interactions tend to form widespread and changing organized patterns without following overall instructions for how the patterns should be organized. To name the systems complex means that they are *unpredictable, non-linear, self-organizing, and emergent*, while being adaptive means that the different agents constrain and adapt their behaviour in relation to other agents. Such computer simulations have provided important theoretical insights into the dynamic behaviour of groups of agents that operate without any central control and with only very simple and local information. By the help of these insights researchers have studied how less advanced living creatures can produce advanced organized patterns, such as ant colonies, schools of fish, and flocks of birds. The results have become part of a wider new paradigm of thought about the complex dynamics of nature, life, and society (see Prigogine & Stengers (1984); Prigogine (1997); and Mainzer (1997) for thorough examinations of the scientific and philosophical foundations, and the implications of complexity thinking).

Since the 1990s, a number of organizational researchers have explored human organizing in terms of complex adaptive systems (Brown & Eisenhardt, 1998; Uhl-Bien, Marion & McKelvey, 2007). However, many of their assumptions overlook important differences in reality between the models, organization in nature, and human organization. Clearly, the organized patterns of behaviour among ants, fish, and birds are simpler than the organized patterns of human social behaviour. Therefore, the models that assume simple and local information are more relevant for the behaviour of simpler organisms. Moreover, computer models are abstract and artificial, and programmed by humans; they are not anything like human reality.

Some earlier contributors (Etzioni, 1961; Czarniawska-Joerges, 1992) to the exploration of organizational complexity have tended to see complexity as that which is complicated or consists of many components. This view rests on the assumption that organizations are complex when a very large number of people interact. Although this might be true, the assumption leaves no explanation of how small groups and individuals can be complex or generate complexity.

Insights from complex adaptive systems research have radically challenged traditional views of complexity. In the computer simulations of interactions between individual agents (which are algorithms) that are not in themselves complex, complex patterns of interaction form whenever the number of agents is medium, in the scale of hundreds, given that they are heterogeneous (Casti, 1994; 1997). A larger number of agents who are homogenous form less complex patterns than a small number of agents who are heterogeneous.

Hence, complexity is primarily associated with heterogeneity and dynamic interaction, not so much with the number of components in a system. A large number of identical agents will only produce static order and repetition. A large number of extreme diverse agents will produce total lack of order, which means that the pattern is not complex but random.

Complexity, then, is created by a dynamic patterning process of local interaction in which *sufficient* variation and numbers of actors are held in paradoxical tension of stability and instability at the same time so that they are able to adapt dynamically to simultaneously form stable and unstable patterns.

Since the beginning of the 2000s other researchers have advanced the use of ideas from complex adaptive systems by combining them with theories and ideas drawn from sociology, psychology, and philosophy (Stacey, 2001; 2010; Griffin, 2002). These researchers have questioned what it means to use the conceptual language of complex adaptive systems to explain phenomena found in human experience. Instead they suggest that this language is used as analogues of human reality, while also proposing that organizations could be seen as *complex responsive processes*.

In this particular theory, attempts are made to link people's interactions and behaviour with change, unpredictability, and experiences of social realities. This is relevant to leaders because it challenges established notions claiming that leaders need to be in control and to manage their organization in order to succeed. From the perspective of complex responsive processes, organized activities are seen as entangled, repetitive, and transformative processes of interaction between people. Individuals, groups, organizations, and societies are seen as different aspects of fundamental processes of communicative interaction. People create and change their complex social patterns of behaviour and experience, their technologies, and their natural environments through these processes of communicative interaction.

Strategies, Leadership, and Complexity

Based on the above outline, my theoretical assumption is that organizations are *paradoxical*, *self-organizing*, and *emergent processes* created in communicative interactions between people. Organizations cannot be subjected to leadership, because organization cannot be separated from leadership. Acts of leadership and/or organization can be performed among people through the influence of themes of communication. When people perform organized activities (i.e. practices), these communicative themes organize their experience of power, belonging (i.e. identity), and ethics.

All individuals' sense of reality is subjective but, at the same time, it is knitted together with and dependent upon other subjective realities in intersubjective processes. In such ongoing processes, the individual and the group are created simultaneously as two sides of the same emerging phenomenon – the organizing social individual.

From this perspective, *strategic and operational decision-making* in the context of organizational response to crisis and emergency are processes that many actors influence based on uncertain and local knowledge rather than on global and certain facts. A *creative strategic response* is the ability to move from static plans (which assumes complete homogeneous actors) towards pragmatic action (which assumes sufficient heterogeneous actors) that will face the immediate situation. Strategy as planned overall direction is transformed to become strategy as emergent coordination of local adaptive patterns of interacting people.

This is the core of the term *emerging strategies*, which means that strategies are not pre-chosen, and sometimes not even known to those who traditionally are charged with making strategies. Patterns of action are bent and sometimes broken completely off from the frameworks of preparations in order to respond to a situation that has not occurred before.

Organizations' abilities to adapt to immediate situations are rooted in organizational practices. It is possible to change and improve those practices because they are created in ordinary everyday activities in organizations that deal with crises and emergencies. At the same time, it is important to recognize that the practices that enable are the same that constrain. Group inclusion cannot happen without group exclusion, hierarchy cannot happen without authority, trust cannot happen outside power relations, and identity cannot happen without difference. These processes and relational phenomena all play a part in constraining and enabling the ability of individuals, groups, organizations, and multiorganizational networks to respond strategically and operationally to crises and emergencies. These ideas are presented and explored in more depth in the theory chapters in Part II and Part III. They form the basis for my theoretical approach to strategies, leadership, and complexity in crisis and emergency operations.

The Research Methodology

The two case studies, which are presented and discussed throughout this book are based on information from interviews, public documents, and media. For the Libya case, interviews were conducted during a 12-month period from the end of the Libya operation in October 2011 through to October 2012, as part of a Royal Norwegian Air Force research project. The interviews included 15 key officers who were part of the military operation. For the police case, 20 people who in different ways were connected to the police operation were interviewed either formally or informally in the course of a four-year period from January 2012 to December 2015.

The analyses are constructed as *interpretative narratives*, with theorizing fused into the material rather than applied instrumentally, meaning that initially the two cases are not subjected to the same thematic and theoretical analysis. I have not aimed at understanding merely the same themes in both cases. Rather, I have been searching for ideas to address particular themes that have stood out in the cases.

The purpose of this approach is to highlight the *differences* between the cases as well as the *similarities*. Regarding differences, for example, the theme of strategy is more salient in the military narrative, whereas the theme of stress is more salient in the police narrative. After the cases have been separately narrated, they are brought together to compare and shed light on their similarities. The theoretical themes are then mobilized into the comparisons of the narratives in order to create new formulations that might clarify shades and nuances in the separate cases, but at the same time also raise doubt on arguments that in each case may have seemed steadfast.

As in any research, there is also here some kind of trade-off. Exploring and comparing the two cases in this book is a choice between pursuing clarity in criteria, facts, and phenomena – much like an investigation commission sets out to do – and accepting that a dynamical approach could at least insert a creativity into the analysis that would allow for nuances in interpretations to emerge even if it means leaving behind any ambition of finding full clarity. The narratives can be told in a number of ways and from different angles and viewpoints, and an endless amount of detail can be emphasized, diminished, made obvious, or made to appear dubious, depending on from which position in the matrix of evolving patterns of events they are viewed and told.

The case stories told here are the author's versions based on the obtained material. Like most people, I was merely a distant spectator of the events when they happened. Thus, the stories are not objective truths; they are outlines of interpretations: versions that can only find validity from the manner in which they are read, perceived, interpreted, and negotiated by those who were close to the events and those of us who were distant from them. Stories are like that – they are constantly reinterpreted by reiteration and by being told in new and different versions.

By gathering the stories and information from selected people who were close to the events, I have tried to get closer to the events than I otherwise would have been able to from merely reading the public documents, media articles, and absorbing broadcasted news and documentaries. However, the sources are ultimately also stories told from particular positions in the event matrix. Not only the involved actor's views but also the documents are constructed within the contextual power constellations through which the events occurred and were made sense of.

In preparing this book, I have encouraged people who participated in the events and people who were distant from the events to read different parts of the manuscript and comment on my interpretations and highlight any obvious errors. Their readings greatly helped me to question and clarify my interpretations. I see this ongoing questioning and challenging of interpretations as part of the politics of methodology and organizational process research. Hopefully, this book will continue to open new questions for its readers.

References

Allen, P. M. (1998). Evolving complexity in social science. In: G. Altman & W. A. Koch (eds). *Systems: New Paradigms for the Human Sciences*. New York: Walter de Gruyter.pp. 3-38.

Boin, A., 't Hart, P., Stern, E. & Sundelius, B. (2005). *The Politics of Crisis Management, Public Leadership Under Pressure*. Cambridge: Cambridge University Press.

Boin, A., 't Hart, P., McConnell, A. & Preston, T. (2010). Leadership Style, Crisis Response and Blame Management: The Case of Hurricane Katrina. *Public Administration*, 88(3), pp. 706–723.

Brown, S. L. & Eisenhardt, K. (1998). *Competing on the Edge: Strategy as Structured Chaos*. Boston, MA: Harvard Business School Press.

Casti, J. (1994). *Complexification: Explaining a Paradoxical World Through the Science of Surprise*. London: HarperCollins.

Casti, J. L. (1997). *Would-Be Worlds*. Chichester: John Wiley & Sons.

Casto, C. A. (2014). *Crisis Management: A Qualitative Study of Extreme Event Leadership*. Dissertations, Theses and Capstone Projects. Paper 626.

Czarniawska-Joerges, B. (1992). *Exploring Complex Organizations*. London: Sage.

Dalal, F. (1998). *Taking the Group Seriously: Towards a Post-Foulkesian Group Analytic Theory*. London: Jessica Kingsley Press.

Elias, N. (1939/2000). *The Civilizing Process*. Oxford: Blackwell.

Elias, N. (1991). *The Society of Individuals*. Oxford: Blackwell.

Etzione, A. (1961). *A Comparative Analysis of Complex Organizations*. New York: The Free Press of Glencoe.

Farazmand, A. (2007). Learning from the Katrina crisis: A global and international perspective with implications for future crisis management. *Public Administration Review*, 67, pp. 149–159.

Griffin, D. (2002). *The Emergence of Leadership: Linking Self-Organization and Ethics*. London: Routledge.

Hannah, S. T., Uhl-Bien, M., Avolio, B. J. & Cavarretta, F. L. (2009). A framework for examining leadership in extreme contexts. *The Leadership Quarterly*, 20(6), pp. 897–919.

Helslott, I., Boin, A., Jacobs, B. & Comfort, L. K. (eds) (2012). *Mega-Crisis: Understanding the Prospects, Nature, Characteristics, and the Effects of Cataclysmic Events*. Springfield, IL: Charles C. Thomas Publishers Ltd.

Holland, J. (1998). *Emergence From Chaos to Order*. New York: Oxford University Press.

House of Commons Foreign Affairs Committee (2016a). Libya: Examination of Intervention and Collapse and the UK's Future Policy Options. Third Report of Sessions 2016–17. Report HC119. London: House of Commons.

House of Commons Foreign Affairs Committee (2016b). Libya: Examination of Intervention and Collapse and the UKs Future Policy Options, Report HC 520. London: House of Commons.

Johannessen, S. O. (2015). Reforming the Norwegian police: Cultural change as a restoration of organizational ideologies, myths and practices. *Nordisk Politiforskning*, 2(2), pp. 167–182.

Johannessen, S. O. & Kuhn, L. (eds) (2012). *Complexity in Organization Studies, Volume I-IV*. London: Sage.

Kadota, R., Varnam, S. & Tokuhiro, A. (2014). *On the Brink: The Inside Story of Fukoshima Daiichi*. Fukuoka: Kurodahan Press.

Kauffmann, S. A. (1993). *Origins of Order: Self-Organization and Selection in Evolution*. Oxford: Oxford University Press.

Maclean, N. (1992). *Young Men and Fire*. Chicago: University of Chicago Press.

Mainzer, K. (1997). *Thinking in Complexity: The Complex Dynamics of Matter, Mind, and Mankind*. 3rd ed. Berlin, Germany: Springer Verlag.

Mead, G. H. (1934). *Mind, Self and Society*. Chicago: Chicago University Press.

NOU (2012). *Rapport fra 22.julikommisjonen. 2012:14.* Oslo: Statens forvaltning-stjeneste. [English version of selected chapters at www.regjeringen.no/html/smk/2 2julikommisjonen/22julikommisjonen_no/en.htm]

Pfeifer, J. W. (2007). Understanding how organizational bias influences first re-sponders at the world trade center. In: B. Bogar, L.M. Brown, L. E. Beutler, J. N. Breckenridge & P. G. Zimbardo (eds). *Psychology of Terrorism.* Oxford: Oxford University Press, pp. 207–215.

Prigogine, I. (1997). *The End of Certainty: Time, Chaos and the New Laws of Nature.* New York: The Free Press.

Prigogine, I. & Stengers, I. (1984). *Order Out of Chaos: Man's New Dialogue With Nature.* New York: Bantam Books.

Rogers, W. P. (Chairman) (1986). *Report of the PRESIDENTIAL COMMISSION on the Space Shuttle Challenger Accident.* June 6th, Washington, DC. http://history.nasa.gov

Rosenthal, U., Boin, A. & Comfort, L. K. (2001). *Managing Crisis: Threaths, Dilemmeas, Opportunities.* Springfield, IL: Charles C. Thomas Publisher ltd.

Schneider, S. K. (2005). Administrative Breakdowns in the Governmental Response to Hurricane Katrina. *Public Administration Review,* 65(5), pp. 515-516.

Stacey, R. D. (2001). *Complex Responsive Processes in Organizations: Learning and Knowledge Creation.* London: Routledge.

Stacey, R. D. (2010). *Complexity and Organizational Reality.* London: Routledge.

Taylor, J. & Van Every, E. J. (2014). *When Organization Fails: Why Authority Matters.* New York: Routledge.

The National Commission on Terrorist Attacks Upon the United States (2004). *The 9/11 Commission Report.* Washington, DC: National Commission on Terrorist Attacks Upon the United States.

The National Diet of Japan (2012). *The Fukushima Nuclear Accident Independent Investigation Commission.* Tokyo: The National Diet of Japan.

Uhl-Bien, M., Marion, R. & McKelvey, B. (2007). Complexity leadership theory: Shifting leadership from the industrial age to the knowledge era. *The Leadership Quarterly,* 18, pp. 298–318.

Weick K. E. (1993). The collapse of sensemaking in organizations: The Mann Gulch disaster. *Administrative Science Quarterly,* 38(4), pp. 628–652.

Weick, K. E. (2001). *Making Sense of Organization.* Malden, MA: Blackwell.

Part I

The Police in National Emergency

2   Terror in Norway[1]

Oslo, 22 July 2011: The Bomb

In the morning and early afternoon of 22 July 2011, the day was calm and relaxed in Oslo, Norway. It was a Friday, at the height of the summer holiday season, and normal working hours in public offices ended at 15:00. Relatively few people were in the Government complex in central Oslo at 15:26, when a major car bomb exploded in front of the 12-storey building that housed the prime minister's offices on the top floors. The bomb destroyed both these and several other offices and buildings in close proximity, including those of the Ministry of Justice, the ministry in charge of the police and internal national security issues.

Prime Minister Jens Stoltenberg was safe in his residence a few blocks away, where he was preparing to speak to his party's youth organization the following day on the island of Utøya.

The Island of Utøya, 22 July 2011: The Mass Shooting

Utøya is a small island of 0.12 square kilometres located in Tyrifjorden, 38 km north-east of Oslo, see Map in Appendix 1, page 155. It has been associated with the labour movement in Norway since 1933 when it was bought by the LO.[2] Back then, it was used among other things as holiday camp for poor children of unemployed workers from Oslo. Since 1950 it has been owned by AUF, the youth organization of the Norwegian Labour Party.[3] Utøya is accessible via road from Oslo and a ferry from a quay area at the mainland that bears no official name. I will refer to the specific ferry quay on the mainland as Utøya mainland quay; see Map in Appendix 2, page 157. On 22 July 2011, Utøya fell within the North Buskerud Police District[4] (hereafter abbreviated as NBPD). The NBPD's headquarters was in the small city of Hønefoss, 20 km by road from Utøya mainland quay.

For a few days every summer, Utøya is brought to hectic life when AUF holds a summer camp. The members, most of whom are in the age range of 15–25 years, gather for different types of activities that are highlighted by a tradition whereby previous and current party leaders, often prime ministers,

speak to the political recruits. The atmosphere is one of high spirit, infor-
mality, and political engagement. When a prime minister visits, the person
is routinely followed and protected by armed, non-uniformed police officers
from the Norwegian Police Security Service (PST). Otherwise, adult volunteers manage security at the summer camp. On 22 July 2011, there were 564
people on the island.

At 17:17, the terrorist who placed the bomb in Oslo arrived at Utøya by
ferry from the mainland. He was dressed as a police officer and armed with
semi-automatic weapons. With a fake police ID card he had convinced the
ferry skipper to take him across to the island. His story was that the police
needed to inform the summer campers there to take security precautions
after the bombing in Oslo. Four minutes after arriving on the island, he
shot and killed his first victim, a former police officer who was serving as a
volunteer camp guard. In the course of the next 21 minutes, between 17:21
and 17:42, the terrorist murdered 42 people, on average two per minute.
The first emergency call from the island received by the NBPD's operations
centre came at 17:25.

At the same time, 23 officers from the Emergency Response Unit[5] (hereafter named with their call sign Delta), conducted search and rescue work
within the bombed buildings in the Government complex in central Oslo. At
the headquarters in Oslo Police District (hereafter abbreviated as Oslo PD)
a police officer in the operational staff received a phone call from his daughter, who was on Utøya: 'Someone is shooting!' she screamed. The officer
immediately handed the phone to the Delta staff officer, who was standing
next to him. By this coincidence, Delta and the Oslo PD operational staff
were informed about the ongoing shootings in their neighbouring district
NBPD at the same time as the first emergency calls reached the NBPD's
operations centre.

The Delta staff officer acted immediately and at 17:30 all available Delta
units in central Oslo had been notified to prepare for transport. Because of
this quick reaction, a total of 26 men in seven car units from the counterterrorism police force headed towards Utøya at 17:33, 12 minutes after the
shooting began on Utøya and five minutes before the first local NBPD police
unit left from Hønefoss. The NBPD had not yet issued any formal request
for Delta's assistance, so at this time NBPD did not know that Delta forces
were coming.

Delta and NBPD were now in a race against time. Between 17:43 and
17:59, no one was killed on Utøya. The killer was searching and hunting for
his next victims. Terrified youths ran off in all directions, trying the best they
could to find hiding places on the small island. Some of them jumped into
the water in an attempt to swim the 625 metres across the shortest stretch
to the mainland. The terrorist fired shots at some of the youths who were
in the water.

At 17:52, the first police unit (call sign P30) from the NBPD arrived at
Utøya mainland quay. The unit consisted of two police officers equipped

for armed response.[6] Crossing over to the island by an ordinary leisure boat would have taken two to four minutes. The officers had a good view towards the camping site Utvika Camping; 460 metres north of Utøya mainland quay. Five boats were visible at Utvika Camping. In addition, there were boats at another quay 180 metres from where the police officers were standing. The two P30 officers did not cross over to Utøya.

At **17:55**, the P30 officers reported to the NBPD operations centre that they feared being shot at and that they were hiding behind a container on Utøya mainland quay. Meanwhile, civilians were preparing leisure boats to go out and rescue those who were swimming from the island.

Out of Oslo, Delta was hindered by heavy traffic, but at **17:57**, their first unit, D36, reported on the NBPD internal communication network that it was approaching. This was the first contact between Delta and the local police. The NBPD's action leader heard this message and called the P30 officers. He ordered them to find boats for Delta. He then notified D36 that Utøya mainland quay was the designated rally point.[7]

Hence, at **18:00** the operation seemed to be fairly coordinated. Local police (P30) was at the rally point, Delta was close to the rally point, the local action leader was preparing to launch a boat and head for the rally point to pick up Delta and/or P30. However, coordination of the police operation soon started to fall apart.

The D36 officers did not know where the crossing to Utøya was, nor were any of the Delta units equipped with GPS maps or detailed printed maps. Just a few hundred metres from Utøya mainland quay, D36 had to stop and ask someone for directions to Utøya. At **18:02**, the unit missed the small road leading from the main road down to Utøya mainland quay. By then, three boats were available in the quay area.

During the next few minutes, all of the following Delta units either passed or decided to leave the designated rally point, from where it would have taken them a mere three-minutes to cross to Utøya by boat. Ultimately, it took Delta a further 30 minutes to stop the terror on the island. At **18:00**, the terrorist had resumed his killing spree. During the next 30 minutes, 27 people died as a result of the terrorist's actions.

At **18:03**, the D36 officers had no idea where they were. They had passed the designated rally point and diverted from the main road down to Utvika Camping, where they again stopped to ask someone if he could help them with directions to Utøya. The Delta unit behind them, D34, had lost sight of D36 and continued north in the direction of the mainland area opposite the neighbouring island of Storøya; see Map in Appendix 2, page 157. D36 and D34 did not communicate. At the camping site, D36 did not ask for boats and did not check whether it was possible to cross to Utøya from there. D36 seemed insistent on finding Utøya mainland quay, yet at the camping site's quay less than hundred metres away from them there were five boats available. The unit turned and drove back in the direction they came from to search for Utøya mainland quay.

At **18:05**, eight minutes after the P30 officers confirmed the order to look for boats for Delta, the officer P30A was on the quay 180 metres south from Utøya mainland quay. He received a boat that came ashore with people rescued from the water. The boat was three metres in length and had a powerful 50-HP engine. There were two other boats at the same quay. In his statement to the 22 July Commission, the officer did not recall having seen the boat in front of him. He did not report or seize boats for the police operation.

The officer P30B was standing on Utøya mainland quay, from where he had a view to both his colleague on the adjacent quay and the marina at Utvika Camping. However, he seemed paralyzed and did not report anything, not even when a motorboat operated by civilians left to meet an approaching rowing boat, which was carrying youths who had managed to escape from the terror on Utøya.

P30B's only message to the NBPD's operations centre was that he was 'on site' to receive Delta. However, he was not on site. He was going to meet Delta on the main road, but was still on the quay. When he arrived on the main road two minutes later, at **18:07**, he had missed the two first Delta units, but was just in time for the arrival of the next four units. They stopped and one of the officers in Delta unit D35 talked to P30B.

According to the D35 officer's statement to the 22 July Commission, P30B reported that there were no boats at Utøya mainland quay, even though he had been observing the area for 10 minutes and many boats had been in sight. A crucial decision was made: including D36, who had now returned from its detour to Utøya camping, five Delta units abandoned the point where the crossing to Utøya is shortest, in favour of rallying 3.6 km farther north, at the mainland opposite Storøya (called Elstangen on the Map in Appendix 2, page 157). Importantly, Delta had no information on available boat resources at Elstangen.

The Delta units arrived at Elstangen at **18:10**, and by sheer luck they were just in time to be spotted by two NBPD police officers on-board an approaching small rubber police boat. One of them was the NBPD's action leader, who was surprised to see Delta at Elstangen, as he thought they would be at the designated rally point that he had confirmed to them at **17:58**. His plan was to pick up P30 – or preferably Delta – at Utøya mainland quay and from there, go straight to Utøya, to stop the terrorist. Now, the police boat diverted to pick up Delta at Elstangen. The boat could carry a maximum of six persons with heavy police equipment. At Elstangen, it was overloaded with 11 men carrying full equipment, two shields, and a rammer.

At **18:17**, the overloaded boat slowly left land. At **18:19**, its engine stopped. The boat was sinking. A civilian boat came to the rescue at **18:21**. However, the mistake was repeated. The civilian boat was designed to carry five people, but Delta overloaded the boat with 10 men. The 'new' boat continued very slowly, but soon it too became unstable and started to capsize. A second civilian boat came to the rescue, and the Delta men divided their group onto the two civilian boats. They were finally ready to go to Utøya piloted by volunteer civilians, who at this point and without any training or concern for their own safety had become logistics spearheads in a Delta counterterrorism operation.

At **18:25**, one hour after the terror started, Delta arrived at Utøya. Terrified and shocked youngsters pointed the police in the directions where they believed the terrorist was located. However, information was contradictory because the terrorist had been moving around the island and had been seen and heard in different places. Shots had been heard coming from different places too. From Delta's perspective, there was still a possibility that there could be more than one terrorist. Some early reports indicated this, although they were not verified. No shots were heard when Delta arrived at Utøya. They divided into two groups and started moving inwards across the island in two different directions. A few minutes later, one of the groups encountered the terrorist. They called out to him to freeze and show his hands. At a distance, they observed wires on his body and for a moment they thought he had a bomb belt. Delta was ready to take a shot to his head. Then, they saw that the wires were actually cables attached to earplugs and a mobile phone; the terrorist had been listening to music while he was carrying out his massacre. The terrorist was arrested at **18:34**. A total of 34 minutes had passed since Delta had initially missed the crossing at Utøya mainland quay, and 42 minutes since the first police unit from NBPD had decided not to cross from the same place. During this time, 27 people were killed.

In total, 77 people were killed in the terrorist attacks in Oslo and on Utøya on 22 July 2011. Of these, 69 were killed on Utøya, 50 of whom were aged 18 years or younger. A further 33 were shot and injured on Utøya. The total number of injured in both attacks was 260, many of whom sustained very serious and permanent injuries.

Notes

1 The sources for this case are the official report from the 22 July Commission (NOU, 2012); records of the 22 July Commission's interviews held with 29 senior leaders and Government politicians, which are kept in the National Archives (www.riksarkivet.no); transcripts from the parliamentary hearings in November 2012 (www.stortinget.no); and the author's interviews with members of the 22 July Commission, the Emergency Response Unit (Delta), and a number of senior police officers who were on duty on 22 July 2011.
2 The Norwegian Confederation of Trade Unions.
3 The official name is Arbeiderpartiet. It is the largest social democratic party in Norway.
4 As a result of the reorganization of the police in the wake of 22 July 2011, the number of police districts has changed from 27 to 12. Since the start of 2016, the NBPD has been part of a larger district called the South-East Police District.
5 The national police force for counterterrorism.
6 The standard armed response equipment was a 9mm Heckler & Koch P30L pistol and a 9mm Heckler & Koch MP5 submachine gun, a bulletproof vest, and a helmet with a protective visor.

7 A rally point is defined as a specific, pre-planned, designated safe area within the response locality, where responders can assemble or regroup as necessary. Security at rally points should be established as a precaution (FEMA, 2000).

References

FEMA (2000). *Emergency Response to Terrorism: Tactical Considerations: Company Officer*. Federal Emergency Management Agency, United States Fire Administration, National Fire Academy.

NOU (2012). *Rapport fra 22. julikommisjonen. 2012:14*. Oslo: Statens forvaltningstjeneste. [English version of selected chapters at www.regjeringen.no/html/smk/22julikommisjonen/22julikommisjonen_no/en.htm]

3 Panic and Collapse of Hierarchy

Making Sense of Organizational Practice

The challenges faced, and the mistakes and decisions made when a police organization responds to large, dynamic, multiple terrorist attacks, such as those in Norway on 22 July 2011 cannot only be reduced to questions of individual judgement and choices. More importantly, we need to ask *how* individuals in such organizations behave and make decisions as part of group patterns and organizational patterns.

In the following I analyse the police response to the terrorist attacks in terms of the dynamic patterns of communication, identity, power, and ethics in groups and organizations, patterns that I shall refer to in this book as *organizational practices*. I also draw on Weick's idea of *sensemaking* (Weick, 2001), and I explore how sensemaking and organizational practices connect in the 22 July case.

Stress and Panic During an Emergency

In stressed situations, according to Weick (1990, 1993), a group can significantly help to reduce anxiety levels, but if that group disintegrates, the relationships that are helpful in making sense of the situation will also disintegrate. Panic will spread as an increased and overwhelming sense of fear, and individuals will be caught in an increasingly stressful pattern in which their consideration for others will become lost in favour of saving themselves. Individuals will revert to unreflective and primitive tendencies to get away from the situation. They will hide or flee from the place or from rational work tasks. Panic will cause the group to dissolve further, which in turn will cause further panic, resulting in a vicious circle.

Panic emerges in contexts where people are confronted with danger that is beyond belief or outside any previous experience they have had. The separation of group members under high levels of stress, even in a group comprising only two members, can release paralyzing reactions. To be paralyzed or consumed by fear is associated with a lack of sensemaking. A person who is left alone is more likely to have problems with creating sense in a situation.

This leads me to the focus of the analysis of the 22 July case: *Which impor-tant moments or situations disrupted the organization, how did it happen, and what were the consequences?*

The first disruptive situation emerged when the senior leaders in the Oslo PD, the National Police Directorate, and the Ministry of Justice acted in response to the bomb in Oslo.

Oslo PD and the National Police Directorate

At all levels of the hierarchy, police officers who were on duty on 22 July were faced with a situation that was far beyond their expectations or previ-ous experience. As their normal organization disintegrated, it became un-clear who was in charge of the various groups and activities. The following narrative of the actions of several key police officers and leaders indicates they were suffering from shock and confusion. They became vulnerable to paralyzing reactions that were amplified by decisions to split up and disrupt the formal organizational structure. This eventually led to a collapse of the operational coordination.

On 22 July 2011, Oslo PD's police chief, Sveinung Sponheim had left his office and was on his way home when he received a call from Oslo PD's operations centre at **15:32**. There had been an explosion in the Government complex: One person was reported killed and there was extensive material damage. In line with standard procedure Sponheim ordered to assemble the Oslo PD's operational staff.[1] When the operational staff is in place, the com-mand structure of the police organization changes. Procedure set the time limit at two hours for establishing the new command structure.

At **15:40**, Sponheim arrived back at Oslo PD's headquarters. He realized at that point that they were facing an act of terrorism. Later, he told the 22 July Commission that his job following the explosion of a terrorist bomb was to describe a scenario to his superiors in the National Police Director-ate (hereafter POD) and then POD's leaders were to assess the situation. However, at **15:46**, 20 minutes after the bomb had exploded, Sponheim had still not contacted his superiors in POD; he had only left a message with a person at POD's emergency call service.

At **16:00**, the situation in Oslo PD's operations centre was chaotic. All lamps were blinking red, overloaded with calls. They needed to prioritize. At this point, Sponheim received information about the perpetrator. At **16:04**, a request to transmit a national alarm and close the borders was sent from Oslo PD's operations centre to the National Criminal Investiga-tion Service (Kripos), the unit in charge of notifying other police districts in cases of national emergency. The request included information about a grey van and the full registration number of that vehicle. By then 40 minutes had passed since the bomb had exploded in central Oslo.

Kripos transmitted the national alarm 40 minutes later, at **16:43**. Odd Reidar Humlegård was the director of Kripos at the time, and he later became the National Police Commissioner. Humlegård informed the 22

July Commission that not much happened during weekends and therefore only one person was on duty at Kripos to deal with the situation on 22 July 2011. When the national alarm was transmitted, the information about the grey van's registration number was incomplete. However, the national alarm turned out to not make any difference to the situation because it was already too late to stop the terrorist from fleeing from Oslo to the site for his next attack.

Back at Oslo PD, Sponheim waited to assemble his operational staff until the tactical commander of the staff turned up at **16:45**. After this, the operational staff failed to put into action the existing plans and procedures for dealing with terror incidents, and they did not prioritize stopping the terrorist from doing more harm. Instead, they concentrated on the rescue work in the Government complex. Sponheim later explained that 'the transition had been fluid' between the ordinary command structure and the crisis command structure. There was no formal transition, so no one knew when and how this had actually happened. By the time the Oslo PD's operational staff started their work – one hour and 20 minutes after the bomb had exploded – the terrorist, Anders Behring Breivik, had already reached Utøya mainland quay, from where a ferry crosses to Utøya.

Operational Leadership Vacuum

Three weeks before 22 July 2011, the acting leader of POD, Deputy National Police Commissioner Vidar Refvik, had signed off and sent out to all police districts a new manual titled *PBS (Police Preparedness System)*. According to this document, in the case of a national emergency event in Oslo, Oslo PD would be defined as the *tactical level* (the lowest level) in the operational hierarchy, POD was defined as the *operational level*, and the Ministry of Justice as the *strategic level*. Despite this theoretical chain of command, Refvik and other senior leaders had great difficulties in putting their own manual's procedures into practice on 22 July.

Refvik did not authorize the activation of POD's counterterrorism and sabotage protocol, because, as he later explained in the parliamentary hearings, he did not think that the explosion was a terror attack. By contrast, at **15:40**, the officer responding to Sponheim's call on POD's emergency phone service was certain that a bomb had caused the explosion. He had intended to notify his leaders of this, but apparently his message did not reach or catch the attention of any of POD's senior leaders.

Instead, the senior leaders of Oslo PD and POD operated independently. Oslo PD's operational staff focused on the rescue work in the bombed area and treated it as a local event, while POD's leaders focused their attention on the hierarchy above them, namely the Government's administrative coordination in national emergencies, called the Government's Crisis Council.

A leadership vacuum emerged at the operational level, where coordination between police districts according to the PBS manual should be carried out. Some leaders were drawn hierarchically upwards to the strategic level and others were drawn downwards towards the local details. As the leaders abandoned their duties to *coordinate* a national emergency response, the operational leadership collapsed both symbolically and in practice. The collapse was represented by total confusion around who was the National Police Commissioner.

Who Was the National Police Commissioner and What Was He Supposed to Do?

The administrative head of the Ministry of Justice, Morten Ruud, was the leader of the Government's Crisis Council on 22 July 2011. He told the 22 July Commission that he was under the impression that the National Police Commissioner Øystein Mæland was operational. He therefore called Mæland at **16:00** and summoned him to the Crisis Council's first meeting, which was scheduled to occur at the Ministry of Defence as soon as the relevant persons could meet. Even though Ruud was Mæland's superior, he did not seem to know that Mæland was on leave at the time and hence not operational.

Moreover, just a few weeks had passed since Ruud and his staff at the Ministry of Justice had appointed Mæland to his position. As a former politician, junior minister, and psychiatrist, Mæland did not have a background or experience in police work. When he was appointed, the political view was that the National Police Commissioner should have his primary loyalty to the political establishment rather than to the police force. The Minister of Justice and the Government at the time had in the years before been in serious political conflicts with the police union. Their political appointment of National Police Commissioner meant that Mæland was not ready to take charge of the 'operational level' in the situation they were facing. However, Ruud wanted Mæland to join the Crisis Council, a strategic body in a national emergency. The notions of where the National Police Commissioner should be clearly differed at the 'operational level' and the 'strategic level'.

While Ruud summoned Mæland to the Crisis Council, Ruud's information chief independently summoned the Deputy National Police Commissioner, Vidar Refvik, to the same meeting. In Mæland's absence Refvik was acting as National Police Commissioner and it was in this capacity he was summoned. Hence, at **16:00**, *two* national police commissioners were summoned to the same meeting at the 'strategic level', where neither of them belonged according to POD's own manual for crisis management.

However, there was still time for them to coordinate their efforts. While on his way to POD's offices, Mæland called Refvik. In their joint testimony to the parliament (Stortinget) in November 2012, both Mæland and Refvik explained that during this phone call they did *not* discuss their individual roles. As a result, Refvik had ended up in the Crisis Council in the role of National Police Commissioner, and Mæland had ended up in POD's operational staff also in the role of National Police Commissioner. According to Mæland's official statement, he himself 'did not have a clue' what was happening there. He was stuck like a 'fish out of water'. Refvik, who was supposed to provide advice to the Crisis Council, was equally unaware of what was going on in POD's operational staff.

Had Mæland and Refvik swopped their whereabouts they would at least have had a chance of contributing to the hierarchical system they had designed. Mæland lacked police experience, but he had extensive political experience, which should have placed him as advisor to his old friend Prime Minister Jens Stoltenberg. Refvik, on the other hand, had spent most of his career in the police. Presumably, in his role of Deputy National Police Commissioner, he could best have contributed to the coordination of the national police resources in the POD's operational staff, and from there he could have informed Mæland and the Crisis Council on a regular basis about key operational decisions.

However, for some reason, Mæland and Refvik swopped jobs, apparently without informing their superiors or discussing the implications. During much of the afternoon and evening of 22 July 2011, in the most challenging crisis and police operation in Norway's recent history, no one, including the Prime Minister, knew who was the National Police Commissioner. In fact, there were two commissioners acting as if they did not even know themselves.

Confusion at a High Level

At **17:00**, Morten Ruud and Vidar Refvik arrived at the Ministry of Defence, where the Crisis Council was to hold its meetings. Refvik was to inform the other members of the council about the ongoing police operation and offer his best police advice to them and the Government. However, he later emphasized several times in his statements that he did not know what was going on in the police operation then or during the afternoon and evening on 22 July, neither from POD's perspective, Oslo PD's perspective, nor from NBPD's perspective.

Prime Minister Jens Stoltenberg also knew very little. Stoltenberg called Refvik directly, even though Refvik ranked five hierarchical levels below the Prime Minister. Stoltenberg told the 22 July Commission that he believed Refvik was the National Police Commissioner. Refvik did not inform Stoltenberg that this was not the case and that the real Commissioner, Mæland, was merely an observer in POD's operational staff.

Refvik told the Commission that instead of focusing on the police operation, he was more concerned with – on behalf of the Prime Minister – stopping a press conference planned by Oslo PD for **17:30**, because the Prime Minister wanted to be the first to inform the public. Without informing his superior, Mæland, Refvik took the role as the Prime Minister's information officer. His strategic and operational leadership duties were at the same time left to collapse together with the organization he was in charge of.

Given his new taken role as information officer, what was the quality of the information that Refvik gave to the Prime Minister? From where did he get the information? According to his own statement, he obtained it from Oslo PD's police chief, Sponheim, yet Sponheim claimed that he did not talk to Refvik on 22 July 2011.

After having participated for over seven hours on the Crisis Council as chief of POD, Refvik returned to POD's offices for a joint meeting at **01:00**. There, for the first time after the bomb had exploded 200 metres from their offices nine and a half hours earlier, the two National Police Commissioners, Mæland and Refvik, finally met.

At **03:50**, Mæland held a press conference and informed that at least 80 people had been *confirmed* killed on Utøya and an additional seven people had been killed in the Government complex in Oslo. At a press conference at **08:00** the next morning, Prime Minister Stoltenberg repeated the same numbers. Just after that, at **09:15**, Oslo PD stated they had confirmed information that 84 persons were dead on Utøya and seven in Oslo. They were not sure if the number in Oslo was correct. In the afternoon on 23 July, the police made a new confirmation, this time the total number of killed persons had risen to 85. Three days later, on 26 July, the police informed that 68 persons had been killed on Utøya, before the correct number of 69 dead on Utøya and eight in Oslo eventually appeared on 27 July.

The Local Police Response to the Attacks on Utøya

The *second* crucial moment of organizational disruption happened as the NBPD responded to the shootings at Utøya.

Sensemaking and Decision-making

Before the attack on 22 July 2011, the local police had not paid any particular attention to the summer camp event on Utøya. There were no briefings earlier in the day of the officers on duty about raised awareness or security issues at the camp. In the NBPD, a geographically large but sparsely populated police district, several of the police officers were not aware that there was a major summer camp that day, nor were they familiar with the location of the island and the surrounding area.

When the terrorist struck and the local police officers were called out, this must have been a surreal experience for them. First the bomb explosion in Oslo, which immediately seemed most likely to be an act of terror, then a second likely act of terrorism had struck on a remote island in their peaceful rural district. The local police were as organization entirely unprepared for this. The risk of some of the police officers panicking was imminent. However, some of the local police officers on duty were qualified to deal with terrorists. The action leader, who was in the second responding unit (P31) out of Hønefoss police station at **17:48**, had a history from the Emergency Response Unit (Delta). His partner in P31 was trained and certified at the highest level of local armed police response (called UEH). However, others, such as the two first responding officers arriving on Utøya mainland quay (P30 A and B), were only certified at the lowest level for armed response.[2]

Weick (2001, pp. 106–108) differentiates between sensemaking and decision-making. Sensemaking is about contextual rationality, of constructing sense into what is going on. It is a process by which people struggle to find meaning in and rationalize what they are doing in response to what they are observing and experiencing. Decision-making is about intended actions to be carried out in the near or distant future. There is always a gap between decisions and actions, but both are in some way related to sensemaking. Before any sense is constructed of a situation, there is no room to make sensible decisions. Actions based on spontaneous decisions made on the grounds of overwhelming feelings of stress and panic without any prior sensemaking are prone to put the organization at risk for at least two reasons.

First, the structure of the organization is dependent on coordinated actions, which is dependent on sense arising in the group of what the actions mean. Sense-less individualized actions can rip the organization apart in fragments. Second, there is the opposite effect on the group. Sense-less group actions can reinforce and create a 'bubble' where the universe by which the group makes sense and decisions shrinks to contain only the group and the immediate cause and effects in the close vicinity of the group, like for instance the extreme actions of a mob. In cases of responses to emergencies, group actions can take the form of the responders rushing into a situation before considering whether that would be sensible.

At the NBPD's operation centre, a situation emerged that would increase the type of vulnerabilities associated with spontaneous decision-making and actions without sensemaking. As the operations centre became inundated with urgent calls, they were handled by a single operator, who made decisions despite not having any possibilities to make sense of the situation. At the same time, in the room next door several of the operator's colleagues were occupied with making sense of the TV news about the Oslo bombing, without having to make any decisions concerning the calls suddenly bombarding the only operator working at the operations centre. From this moment, the organization collapsed rapidly in the absence of leadership. Weick states:

> When a formal structure collapses, there is no leader, no roles, no routines, no sense.
>
> (2001, p. 115)

The NBPD police chief, Sissel Hammer, was away on a tour of her district on 22 July. She was new in her job and had not rehearsed routines for the operational staff or other procedures for major events in her district. While in her car, she was called from Oslo PD and told that Delta was on its way.

She was told to organize her operational staff. She could not. Her colleagues did not call her, and she was decoupled from the operation until she arrived at the headquarters after the arrest of the terrorist.

Loss of Meaning and Structure

During an emergency, panic erupts when an organization starts to disintegrate. At the NBPD, this happened around 17:30, when people were thrown into different tasks to stop a terrorist attack, despite the lack of preparation, a plan, or proper coordination. As the organization fell apart, and the levels of stress and panic increased, the organization disintegrated even further.

Weick (2001, p. 105) in his Mann Gulch analysis of the disintegrating organization of a group of fire fighters pointed to the risks of such organizational disruption during life-threatening situations. A group, no matter how small, increases the chances of making sense of the situation and by this the chances to make sensible decisions. Counter to this, the disintegration of a group's cohesion leaves the individual stripped from any means of making sense in a chaotic, senseless, and life-threatening context.

In the Mann Gulch case, the firefighters lost contact with their leader. In what Weick calls the 'role system', their place and identity as part of the organization fell apart (ibid, p. 108). Similarly, in the 22 July event, several of the local police units from the NBPD as well as Delta lost contact and coordination with the NBPD operations centre, their incident commander, and their action leader. Orders were given and forwarded by different leaders without clear confirmation. The 22 July Commission states that as late as 18:09 there was chaotic activity on the communication network, with police officers asking for confirmation of the rally point without getting it.

For the two frontline police officers (P30 A and B) arriving at Utøya mainland quay 22 minutes after the initial emergency calls from Utøya, the experience must have been overwhelming. They soon showed signs of panic, confusion, and evasive behaviour.

The Partners

For P30, the chance of sensemaking largely depended on them sticking together. However, after taking cover together behind a container for five minutes, they split up. Both officers were now left alone to make further sense of what was happening and how, as police officers, they could fit into the chaotic and highly uncertain universe in which they suddenly found themselves. Left on their own, they were in a situation that did not resemble anything in their previous experience. It would likely have been unclear for them what would be meaningful actions and working tasks. Their possibility of making sense of the situation and discussing sensible actions was lost when they lost contact with each other. In such situations, people might regress to first learned behaviour (Barthol & Ku, 1959).

In the case of P30, first learned behaviour, as local police officers, is to observe, provide help, and interfere in low-risk situations, not to confront terrorists in a war-like fashion. P30A directed his attention away from confronting the terrorist as he went to the neighbouring quay to help those who had escaped from the island. For him, it must have made sense to take the role of *rescuer*. P30B stood frozen for seven minutes in observational fixation. Time and space seemed to stop, as he became an *observer* of the events. As police officers with a duty to stop crime, P30's purpose and identity collapsed in relation to the reality of the situation. Their attention shifted from the high-risk to the low-risk end of being a police officer as they turned to undertake less dangerous tasks away from the frightening idea of immediately having to go to the island.

When P30 split up it might have seemed like a small change. However, in the particular context in which they only had each other to make sense of the chaos, splitting up was a potential recipe for intense and heightened feelings of stress. In his statement to the 22 July Commission, one of the officers said that he felt a sense of hopelessness. It must have been more than that because he did not recognize the incoming boat at the spot where he was standing as a potential resource for a police operation. In fact, he claimed he did not recall having seen it at all.

The 22 July Commission criticized the two P30 officers for not attempting to cross to the island. According to the Commission, it would have been possible for P30 to be on the island as early as **18:00** had they been properly coordinated and decisive, in which case they would have been there in time to interfere with the terrorist's second wave of killings between **18:00** and **18:30**, a wave that left 27 people dead in addition to the 42 he killed earlier. The Commission argued that the officers had failed to adhere to what the law refers to as police officers' general 'duty to act' to stop crime. The police officers argued that from their arrival at Utøya mainland quay at **17:52** they had just followed orders to stay on the mainland and observe until backup resources arrived.

However, they did not follow the orders they received. The Commission stated: 'the Commission's view is that P30's situation changed when they received their orders to find boats for Delta. Their lack of engagement in securing boats between **17.57** and **18.15** was not in line with the orders' (NOU, 2012, p. 133, my translation). The first order, at **17:51**, was to observe. However, instead of observing, they hid behind a container and were unable to observe boats in the area. The second order, at **17:57**, was to find boats for Delta. That order was not pursued either. Even when one of the officers helped receive escapees from the island who arrived by boat at **18:00**, he did not report the boat as a resource for Delta.

Upon their arrival at Utøya mainland quay, the P30 officers must have been terrified. As civilians rescued people from the water, P30 took refuge behind a container and reported they were afraid that they could be shot. Clearly, their stress levels were high. Stress levels might have been reduced when they were safe behind the container together. When the second order reached them, they might have been relieved to learn that Delta was coming to help them, because shortly after they emerged from behind the container and into open terrain. However, they then split up. As they were splitting up, they would have heard rounds of heavy gunshots at the island at **18:00** as the terrorist started his second wave of killings. Separated from each other, this probably would have escalated their feelings of stress and panic to a level where the order to find boats for Delta could have been suppressed and difficult to turn into rational action.

The P30B officer froze for seven crucial minutes at the quay before making his way to the main road to meet Delta. As a result, he missed the first two units, D36 and D34. They each arrived there with a total of eight men at **18:01** and **18:03**, respectively. Both units missed the diversion at the main road and continued farther north. Had P30B been there, it is possible that D36 and D34 would have gone to the ferry quay, because D36's clear understanding at that time was that the quay was the rally point. In their testimony to the Commission, the D36 officers stated that they would have crossed from this site had they known where the crossing was and been given access to boats. Such scenario would have made it possible for Delta to arrive at the island 15–20 minutes earlier than they actually did.

Notes

1 A police district's operational staff is a formal structure put into place only in case of large or serious incidents. Their role is strategic coordination of operational resources while an operations centre with its leader takes charge of the tactical operation.
2 Norwegian police is normally non-armed but trained for armed response at different levels. Local police are certified at two levels. Most police officers are certified to the lowest level, allowing them to be armed for assignments of low risk and complexity, while 15–20% of local operational police officers are trained at the highest local level (UEH), enabling them to handle more complex armed operations. The Emergency Response Unit, Delta, is a national resource trained at the highest level, which means that they are expected to undertake all types of armed police operations, including high-risk complex counterterrorism operations all over the country.

References

Barthol, R. P. & Ku, N. D. (1959). Regression under stress to first learned behaviour. *Journal of Abnormal and Social Psychology*, 59, pp. 134–136.
NOU (2012). *Rapport fra 22.julikommisjonen. 2012:14.* Oslo: Statens forvaltningstjeneste. [English version of selected chapters at www.regjeringen.no/html/smk/22julikommisjonen/22julikommisjonen_no/en.htm]
Weick K. E. (1990). The vulnerable system: An analysis of the Tenerife air disaster. *Journal of Management*, 16(3), pp. 571–593.
Weick K. E. (1993). The collapse of sensemaking in organizations: The Mann Gulch disaster. *Administrative Science Quarterly*, 38(4), pp. 628–652.
Weick, K. E. (2001). *Making Sense of Organization.* Malden, MA: Blackwell.

4 Collapse of Leadership and Coordination

In this chapter, I continue with the third and fourth crucial moments of organizational disruption in the 22 July case. The *third* moment was the decision to change the rally point from Utøya mainland quay to Elstangen, 3.6 km farther north. Why and how did this happen?

The Misunderstanding

Before considering these questions, let us first consider the information that was available to the 22 July Commission when they assessed the decision to change the rally point. The Commission accessed recorded logs from the NBPD's internal communication network. However, the communication network was of poor quality and many police officers used mobile phones to communicate. The Commission did not access the police officers' mobile phone logs.

In addition, crucial information was exchanged face to face between police officers. Information from some of those exchanges was accounted for in the interviews held by the Commission, but they were not reliable. Different actors had different versions of what had been said. Moreover, many of the people involved were never interviewed because the Commission only selected those it believed would provide sufficient information for its mandate to be fulfilled.

The Commission's mandate and objective was to clarify how the terrorism acts could have been avoided in the months and years before 22 July 2011, to clarify what actually happened that day, and to identify aspects within the Government's area of responsibility that could represent lessons learned for prevention and response to any future terror attacks. The Commission was given full authority to access any information it needed. However, it did not conduct a criminal investigation into negligence or failures to carry out responsibilities, and it did not attempt to explain in any detail how and why the police organization collapsed.

In the interviews held by the Commission, the witnesses were asked to share any information they had in relation to the events on 22 July 2011. The interviews with Delta members were conducted several months after this day. In the meantime, Delta officers had coordinated their explanations as a result of their routine stress management work. This work, which is psychologically and operationally important for the members to make sense of their experiences, inevitably also coordinated each member's understanding of what happened.

Delta's internal evaluation report was released on 21 October 2011. The Commission's interviews were held after that date, and with the Delta chief as late as March 2012. Delta is a very closed group, in which all members depend on each other. They are trained for high-risk operations where their lives depend on the group support. Its most important explicit value is the united group in the spirit of 'one for all and all for one'. In the interviews with the Commission held after Delta had delivered their official report, it is very unlikely that the Commission would have heard any significant variations in the Delta officers' explanations and stories. Their main story was that their units had received the order from the NBPD's operations centre to rally on Elstangen near Storøya. By contrast, the NBPD claimed that Delta had made the decision. The Commission concluded that there had been a *misunderstanding*.

This demonstrates clearly that the decision was not isolated to an individual in the hierarchy. Could it be possible that no single leader made the decision to change the rally point, but that everyone went there because they thought 'the others' would, similar to the phenomenon described by Harvey (1974) as the Abilene paradox?[1]

Mead's Ideas of Communication

If we turn to G. H. Mead's ideas of communication as *social acts* (Mead, 1934), a key insight is that meaning emerges in the act of gesture and response, in which the gesture is, for example, when someone's words are spoken in a particular context. Feelings and tone of the voice cannot be separated from what is spoken. However, the *meaning* of what is spoken will emerge when another person responds in the same context in his or her own words, feelings, and tone, and the first person responds to that, and so forth. In this ongoing social act, the meaning of what they are communicating emerges for the participants. Since they have different life histories, experiences, knowledge, and ways of interpretation, they will inevitably understand what is going on in different ways.

When people act as if they understand each other, it is on the basis of their experience of being capable to perform coordinated actions in relation to each other, not on the basis that they understand identically what is going on. It follows that we can only rely on what we, in our experience, have learned to understand. Experience tells us that we are able to coordinate to get things done, and when collaborative work is flowing, we might think that all persons involved understand the situation the same way. However, the paradox is that experience also tells us that in organizations many complicated coordinated actions are performed even when people are in conflict with each other and even if people lack the overview they are told they should have or that they pretend to have.

Coordinated social acts thus happen when people understand each other sufficiently well to move on to their next action. As actions and interactions evolve, the actors will discover that many of the things they do are similar in similar situations. They experience coordination even if they understand situations differently. Thus, human beings who are in similar contexts are capable of understanding and acting in similar, but not identical, ways in relation to other human beings. Social acts are paradoxical because coordination happens as a result of both *differences* and *similarities* between the actors. The paradox creates flexibility, which is a prerequisite for coordination. Coordination is therefore an activity that involves conflict. Furthermore, even when people act collaboratively, they may differ in their understandings.

Hence, Mead explained a universal human experience: we are able to coordinate and act as a group at the same time as we are able to act in variation as individuals and to break a group's pattern. If we did not perform this ability, there would be no formation of different groups or group diversity. We are able to repeat actions so that we can both shape structure and anticipate what is going to happen next, thereby enabling us to make sense of our experience. At the same time, we are able to create novelty – things that have never been there before – and hence develop and evolve our actions and interactions even further. We are able to say to each other that we understand each other, and we can empathize and sympathize by taking the position of the other (person and group) to ourselves. At the same time, we experience that we can misunderstand and end up in conflicts based on diametrically opposed views and understandings of a situation.

Taking Mead's ideas into account implies that misunderstandings are *normal* ways of communicating, not expressions of bad or wrong ways of communicating. Misunderstandings are important in the sense that they are expressions of creativity and fantasy. They are imaginative interpretations, which function to serve flexibility and the creation of novelty (Fonseca, 1998). At the same time, what is new is not necessarily good or efficient. If the decision to go to Elstangen was a result of a misunderstanding, it probably delayed the police operation. However, there is no way of knowing what would have happened if the police had not gone to Elstangen. Perhaps, then, other misunderstandings would have delayed and altered the course of the operation in ways we cannot imagine.

Different Meanings of Misunderstanding in Different Practices

Misunderstanding applies also to how the term itself can have different meanings, and hence be misunderstood in different organizational practices.

Interestingly, the operational police, both Delta and the NBPD's operations centre, rejected the suggestion that there had been a misunderstanding between them. Power and prestige entered into the understanding of communication. They all wanted to give the impression that they had followed procedure, that the hierarchy was in place, that they were in control, and that the communication on the particular issue of rally point was clear. Their understanding of communication was an instrumental sender-receiver understanding where messages and orders are sent by a sender to be received by a receiver, who then would understand the message in the same way as the sender (Shannon & Weaver, 1949).

From this perspective, if both parties do not understand the message in the same way, one or both parties are failing in their responsibilities or communication abilities. Communication is then an individual act, not a social act. The individual who speaks is responsible for clarifying the meaning of the message and the receiver is responsible for asking the sender to repeat the message with more clarity if the message is not clear enough.

In many operational organizations, procedures for using two-way radio communication are based on this mechanical sender-receiver idea with the aim of avoiding misunderstandings. The person at the receiving end will respond with short, standardized, and sometimes coded words (e.g. 'standby', 'affirmative', 'negative', 'roger', 'repeat').

Sometimes a message or an order will be repeated word by word, thus giving the impression that repetition of words means there is clarity and identical understanding. The reasoning behind such communication practices is that there could be major negative consequences in an operation if someone has misunderstood a message or an order and at the same time has failed to do enough to clarify it.

In the Tenerife air disaster, for example, the communication between the control tower and the captains and co-pilots leading to the disaster was described as a series of misunderstandings (Weick, 1990). For boards doing inquiries into major accidents or events, misunderstandings in themselves are seen as causes of flawed actions, typically when it is difficult to be clear about individual responsibility or negligence. Misunderstanding is in such cases another expression of the normal emergent results of social interaction that might lead to what Perrow (1984) called normal accidents.

Dekker (2012) argues that we need to move away from a culture where individuals are blamed for accidents, to a more balanced and negotiated view. The understanding underlying this view is that accidents cannot be referred back to a single person or component in a linear cause-effect explanation, and that analysis and investigations into accidents and catastrophic events would benefit from a complexity theoretical approach (Dekker, Cilliers & Hofmeyr, 2011). Persons are integrated into organizational and technological complexities, which by their interactions amplify errors in a way that might spiral non-linearly out of control and cause major accidents and breakdowns of organization.

The 22 July Commission stated they were not looking for scapegoats. The Commission seemed to be aware of the power of public scrutiny and raised concern about *external* blame cultures manifested by public inquiries and investigations. However, we see in the 22 July case how an *internal* blame culture in the police emerged when the external Commission moved away from blaming one person or group. We also see why an internal blame culture in group-oriented operational practices might function as protection of the group and the organizational hierarchy.

From the viewpoint of professional operational actors, any competent and responsible professional must do everything to avoid misunderstandings. For operational actors, the meaning of messages sent and received is seen as something that should suppress normal interaction to become unequivocal and identical for the actors involved, even though they might find themselves in situations where they must communicate with people from different cultures, with different languages, states of mind, training, and backgrounds.

Misunderstandings challenge the individual performance culture and professionalism of operational groups. Misunderstandings are risks, the sources of failure and disaster. Misunderstandings are outside any operational actor's control and cannot be explained and understood even though they can function to defuse any individual blame. When the failure becomes public, and cannot be isolated to individuals in the hierarchy, it is turned into a group failure. Hence, if the conclusion from external investigations is that a misunderstanding has occurred, the operational groups will have failed without knowing why.

Each involved group will then locate the reason or responsibility for the misunderstanding in another group's action, not their own. It is a way of surviving as a group with their collective and unresolved guilt. Perhaps that is why public exposure of failure explained as misunderstanding was not acceptable to the operational police groups?

Both Delta and the NBPD's operations centre rejected the Commission's suggestion that a misunderstanding in communication between them led to the decision to change the rally point on 22 July 2011. Instead, they blamed each other for not being clear enough and, more importantly, they blamed each other for making what others criticized as the wrong decision about the rally point.

By contrast, the Commission was reluctant to blame the decision on one person or group. Their mandate was explicitly not to look for individual scapegoats. Operating partly within a juridical bureaucratic practice and partly within a political practice, it ended up criticizing the decision to rally on Elstangen, but at the same time concluding that no one was to blame for the decision. Perhaps the Commission thought of this as a compromise that everyone could live with? It was letting the operational actors 'off the hook' while communication in itself, as if it were something happening outside the communicating actors, was given the blame.

However, for the operational police, this was an insult. For them, a person or a group was responsible for the rally point decision. This person or group clearly could be found within the police hierarchy.

The problem was that there were two hierarchies. In the formal hierarchy, the NBPD's operation centre was to blame, whereas in the expert hierarchy Delta was to blame. As Taylor & Van Every (2014) explain, authority is often seen as flowing along the two organizational axes of formal position and expertise. Conflict of authority exists as a constant between these two in modern professional organizations. In the conflict between Delta and the NBPD, the Commission avoided passing judgement. Although a misunderstanding settled the matter for the public and political interests, it was not acceptable for the operational police.

The conflict was clearly visible. Both Oslo PD's and NBPD's reputation were at stake. In the interviews conducted by the Commission, the NBPD's police chief Sissel Hammer accused Delta of getting in the way of the local police operation. She claimed that the NBPD had not asked for assistance and could have handled the situation on Utøya. When this accusation became public in 2012, the Oslo PD police chief, who also is in charge of Delta, publically corrected Hammer and reminded her that the Utøya operation was her responsibility and that she had accepted Delta when Oslo PD called her on 22 July. She could have declined to accept Delta's assistance if she thought it was not needed.

Improvisation: Delta's Decision-making?

So what happened when the decision to change the rally point was made? From interviews and statements made by the Delta chief to the Commission, the media, and to this author, it seems likely that Delta's two main criteria for coordination of operations – a safe rally point and access to necessary resources (in this case boats) – were not clear to any of the Delta units at 18:07 when four of them stopped near Utøya mainland quay to talk to P30B. However, there is no information to suggest that the four units did not know they were at the point of the shortest crossing to the island.

One of the officers in the unit D35 knew the area to some extent and Delta's action leader had assigned him the task of coordinating the rally point with the local police. Ten minutes earlier, at 17:57, there had been phone contact between this officer and the NBPD's operations centre. During this exchange, the NBPD's operator communicated that the rally point was 'down by the quay', which she later claimed was referring to Utøya mainland quay. The D35 officer responded by asking 'The quay by the golf course?' meaning the quay on Elstangen. The NBPD operator took the Delta officer's question as a decision.

However, she did not confirm back that Elstangen was the rally point, even though the D35 officer seemed to have expected verification when he was trying to clarify her message in their exchange. Nor did she notify the

NBPD's incident commander about the change of rally point. If the sender (D35) made a decision without verification, and the receiver (operations centre) accepted the decision without verifying it, while the NBPD's incident commander was not informed at all, it seems both D35 and the NBPD operator had failed to communicate in accordance with hierarchical procedure. There was a double mistake, not a misunderstanding.

However, D35 might not have seen the rally point as fixed at that point in time. The fact that D35 and three other units stopped close to the original rally point and talked to P30B 10 minutes *after* the alleged misunderstanding with the NBPD's operations centre implies that they needed more information and did not want to rely on an unconfirmed rally point. They knew they were preparing for a challenging counterterrorism operation, and they had to decide or make sense of whatever they deemed supportive of their mission.

When stopping to talk to the P30B officer, Delta therefore would have been interested in information about the two things that were decisive for their operation – boats and rally point. According to P30B's statement to the Commission, it was his understanding at that time that Utøya mainland quay was the rally point for the tactical operation. His order was to direct Delta from the main road down to the quay area and to stop any other traffic getting in their way. It seems unlikely that he would have told Delta to continue farther north and, by implication, to change the rally point. Even if he did this, why would Delta have accepted this suggestion without coordinating it with the operations centre?

P30B might have expressed uncertainty about the boat resources available in the vicinity of the quay. After all, he had not managed to fulfil the order to find boats for Delta. Delta claimed he told them there were no boats. The boats were available, however, but both P30 officers seemed to have had difficulties absorbing and making sense of the resources near the quay area, most likely because of psychological stress reactions.

Whatever P30B conveyed to Delta, it is reasonable to assume that Delta was trained to assess critically any information they acquired in stressful contexts. This suggests that, for Delta, at **18:07** the situation was *undecided* about the rally point and the boat resources, and that its units were still seeking clarification. They were not operating on the grounds of a misunderstanding, but rather in their own *modus operandi*. They regarded the local police as unreliable and stressed. The information from NBPD was contradictory. Just one minute after Delta's communication with the operations centre had suggested Elstangen as rally point, the NBPD action leader had called Delta and specifically said that Utøya mainland quay was the rally point.

It is conceivable that P30B could have told them there *were* boats available, but the fact that two Delta units (D36 and D34) had moved on made the next four units weary of splitting the total force. What if D36 and D34 were already preparing to cross from a point ahead and the next four units did not show up to back them? Then they would end up going to the island uncoordinated in different groups, which under certain conditions would carry the potential of them mistaking their own group with the enemy. After all, the terrorist was reportedly dressed as a police officer and they could not rule out more than one terrorist. A choice had to be made between splitting the units and holding them together.

When the Delta units did not get the information they needed from NBPD, they decided to act on their own. They collected whatever information they could on the ground (from P30B), decoupled themselves from the local police, prioritized keeping their own forces together and moved in the direction of Elstangen to join the D34 unit that was already there, albeit by mistake. They based what they did on what they knew and thought was best for them.

A hypothesis suggesting that the Delta units improvised their operations is supported by the fact that, from the outset in Oslo, they responded without any request for assistance from the local police on the basis of the information received from the daughter of a police officer. Then they bypassed the formal hierarchy and presumed that the local police force would adapt to the Delta units on the basis of their superior status in that particular situation.

Delta unit D36's behaviour at Utvika Camping, where it stopped after first having passed Utøya mainland quay, can arguably be seen to strengthen the improvisation hypothesis. Paradoxically, the unit told the Commission it was ready to cross wherever it could find boats, regardless of a rally point, yet strangely it did not ask about boats but for information about the nearest place to cross to Utøya when it was at Utvika Camping.

By contrast, their colleagues in D35 claimed they had asked about boats and not the rally point when they stopped to talk with P30B at almost exactly the same time as D36 was at the camping site. D34 had reached Elstangen at the same time without knowledge of any access to boats there. The D34 officers did not know that Elstangen was in the process of becoming the rally point.

Clearly, D34, D35, and D36 were uncoordinated and acting in an ad hoc manner. Similar to the NBPD units, the Delta units that were supposed to make decisions about the rally point, crossing point, and boat resources were separated from their larger group and from each other. They seemed to operate under very elevated levels of stress, because their behaviour did not match their trained principles.

Delta officers are trained very similarly to military special forces. In the military, techniques for sustaining capability, survival, and pursuing a mission under difficult conditions always include high awareness of exploiting access to useful resources. Utvika camping is right by the water. It was a tremendous resource with a number of boats easily accessible at a marina, and with many people willing to help. Strangely, D36 drove down to the camping site looking for the rally point, but did not recognize the site as a resource.

Instead, at **18:06**, D36 left the hub of resources at Utvika camping and returned along the main road towards Utøya mainland quay, where the unit met the next four Delta units. It then turned once more and followed the four units past the resources at Utvika camping and onwards to Elstangen. D34 had arrived at Elstangen around **18:07**, and the next five units arrived around **18:11**.

Hence, within the fragmented Delta groups there was not *one* decision about a changed rally point, but *three*: first, D34's decision that was likely a result of a mistake where they lost contact following D36; second, the four units including D35 likely made their decision because they had to choose between unreliable NBPD information and catching up with the two other Delta units to keep their force together; and third, D36's decision was likely just to follow the group of four units without really knowing where they were going. The decision to change the rally point to Elstangen was fragmented within the Delta force's own units.

However, there is no clear answer to the role of P30B in the decision to change the rally point. The details of the conversation between D35 and P30B are not known. The conversation might have influenced the decision to change the rally point or it might have confirmed a biased assumption about Elstangen given that D35 knew about the place from before. Perhaps P30B tried to cover over that he had not managed to fulfil the order to find boats for Delta by telling Delta there were no boats there, or perhaps he told Delta there were boats, but Delta chose to follow their own logic. Perhaps the conversation had no effect at all on the decision about rally point.

The Delta force's search for a rally point and boat resources, and their hesitation near the shortest crossing point, indicates that they had two unconfirmed options for rally points as late as **18:07**. It also indicates that they had stress reactions. Whatever made them decide to go to Elstangen, there is no doubt that it was the Delta units' decisions that changed their own rally point, not a decision by the NBPD and not a misunderstanding like the 22 July Commission stated.

Delta at Elstangen

The *fourth* important moment of organizational collapse happened when the Delta units prepared the boats that would take them to Utøya.

After the Delta units ended up 3.6 km farther away from the shortest mainland crossing point, they became painstakingly aware that the force was losing time while the killing continued on the island. The whole force was now together and the group cohesion was further tightened to the point that it left the group unable to diversify. Consequently, the group members first overloaded a police boat, which stopped and almost sank. After their rescue by a volunteer's boat, the group repeated the mistake and had to be rescued yet again, this time by another volunteer's boat. In hindsight, neither Delta nor the 22 July Commission had any language to describe why this happened. Delta referred to it as 'overeagerness', an explanation that was accepted by the Commission without any further discussion.

There were major problems of leadership and acts of coordination within the Delta group, between the Delta group and its command in Oslo, between Delta and the NBPD's operations centre, between the NBPD's operations centre and its leaders, and between the NBPD's operations centre and the Oslo PD's operational staff. As a result, Delta had poor intelligence information and, according to their statements, acted upon unverified information of three to five terrorists on the island.

Confronted with the deadliest danger they ever had faced, the group seemed to regress into overlearned patterns of behaviour, which concerned the safety and protection of the group. If there were five terrorists on the island, two Delta officers for each terrorist would have meant they needed a force of 10 men to go together. They loaded the boat with 10 men in addition to the skipper. The problem with this explanation is that information of more than one terrorist was never confirmed or mentioned by anyone on the police network. All the information from the island that was distributed on the police network about the terrorist(s) referred to one person dressed as a police officer.

Another explanation for the overloading of the boat is that it was a response to elevated stress levels, which the group members must have felt. It tightened the group and reduced levels of creativity and variation. Delta claimed it had followed standard operational procedure, but the question is whether the situation on Utøya demanded more than standard procedure. Could it be that the close-knit group was caught in the phenomenon of 'groupthink'?

Groupthink: Power Dynamics in Groups

Groupthink (Whyte, 1952; Janis, 1982) emerges when only the most practiced and conforming patterns of actions – the habits and routines – can be performed, regardless of the situation. Important information disappears from sight, and everything that supports what appears to be the safest solution is seen and interpreted, but nothing else. This is a stress syndrome, which has some similarities to panic, but where the group conforms rather than disintegrates. Did the Delta force conform due to this stress syndrome during the police operation on 22 July 2011?

The descriptions of Delta's behaviour fit the descriptions of the preconditions and phenomenon of groupthink given by Janis (1982). Janis points to *three preconditions* for a group having a high risk of groupthink: *first*, the group cohesiveness is more important than the individual's right to express an opinion; *second*, structural faults, such as insulation of the group, lack of impartial leadership, and homogeneity of the members' social background and ideology; and *third*, a situational context with highly stressful external threats, excessive difficulties in decision-making, and moral dilemmas (e.g. whether to save lives at the risk of being killed). Arguably, all three preconditions were present as part of Delta's group dynamics on 22 July 2011.

In principle, group members are recruited to Delta from the whole police force, but the selection process deems that they will end up as members of a homogenous group. Delta is the only Norwegian police unit trained as a paramilitary unit. They are tasked with doing whatever it takes to overcome the opponent, to follow orders, and not to express opinions during operations. In their daily activities, the members of the group are mainly isolated from other police units, with one clear decision-maker – the leader of the force.

Delta's training is carried out in very close collaboration with the Norwegian Special Operations Commando, the military special forces branch on standby for both national and international counterterrorism and other special operations. In the same way as their military colleagues, much of their activity is encapsulated in secrecy and mythology. For ordinary police officers, this has led to a heroic aura around Delta: they are regarded as capable of doing anything they are assigned to do. Within the group, Delta members are very competitive and have high expectations of their performance skills. The group culture clearly leans towards an overestimation of the group's power and morality, internal pressure for uniformity, and tailored mindsets, which are exactly the categories Janis described as symptoms of groupthink.

The Identity Narrative of Delta: Hostage Situations and Superiority

According to a statement from their chief, Delta did not see the Utøya situation as any different from any other hostage situation. Perhaps this comparison can tell us something about their behaviour on 22 July 2011? Delta is trained for high-risk operations, but among these situations hostage-taking represents a lower risk to them than ongoing shooting. In a hostage situation, they can normally isolate the context and to a greater extent plan their actions. Life-threatening risks are higher for the hostages and the hostage-takers than for the police.

In the hostage situations used by terrorists in the 1970s police often tried to negotiate with the terrorists for time and minor exchanges between the parties. For the police, it was an important tactic because the hostage situation at the outset is a stalemate, a confrontation between the police and the terrorists where no party can proceed without putting the lives of the other party, and the hostages, at risk. The only way out for the police is to gain time, keep the negotiations going, and prepare to make a surprise attack. The hope is that at some point the hostage-takers will give themselves up. Alternatively, if it becomes necessary, the police will proceed with a surprise attack when the terrorists are tired and off guard.

In the wake of the experiences of hostage situations and other terrorist attacks in the 1970s, counterterrorism special police tactics and training that would emphasize negotiations and surprise attacks were increasingly professionalized in Europe and elsewhere. The Emergency Response Unit (Delta) in Norway was established in 1976 as part of this international development.

One identity-forming story that is circulating within Delta and the ordinary police, and that also is told in a number of ways outside the police (even in a film) concerns a hostage situation in 1994. During an armed robbery, two robbers took three hostages, among them a police officer, in a hijacked escape car. The car ended up at a small airport south of Oslo, where the hostage-takers threatened to kill the hostages if not given USD 10 million and granted safe passage. A local police officer negotiated with the hostage-takers through the police radio of the officer who was taken hostage. When the radio's batteries ran out, the negotiator agreed to bring them new batteries, but he was taken as the fourth hostage.

This was the first real test of its type for the Delta forces. As they surrounded and stalled the situation, a Delta marksman took up position. A side window of the car had a 5-cm opening through which he could see the back of the head of one of the hostage-takers. As the situation deteriorated and demands were not met, the hostage-takers became increasingly aggressive. One of the hostage-takers was holding the fourth hostage (the police negotiator) at gunpoint, forcing him to start the countdown to his own execution aloud over the police radio if the hostage-takers' demands were not met.

With only two minutes left, Delta was given a 'green light' from the local chief of police in charge of the operation to launch its action plan. This marked the first time in Norwegian peacetime history that a police chief had given an order to shoot to kill. Minutes later the operation was over. From a far range, the Delta marksman shot one of the hostage-takers in the head through the 5-cm car window opening and killed him instantly, while an armed Delta vehicle accelerated and rammed the front of the hostage-takers' car at the same time as other Delta officers stormed the car from an adjacent building, rescuing the hostages and arresting the second hostage-taker.

This story is told as a heroic example of a Delta operation that was done by the book with respect to an evolving hostage situation. It serves as an ideal for precision and professionalism, but also as a myth in terms of Delta's superiority over the local police. It is noteworthy how the story includes the image of a 'stupid' local police officer being captured by the hostage-takers, and Delta being decisive and prepared to make the ultimate sacrifice of executing a person in order to save the life of that officer and the other hostages.

Unfortunately, Utøya was outside the range of such Delta mythology. The Delta units did not have a designated rally point or control over the context. Moreover, they did not have time to negotiate with the terrorist, nor did they have any tactical plan. Instead, they were facing an uncontrolled dynamic situation in which defenceless people were systematically hunted and executed on a remote island. The most trained hostage tactics of Delta could not be of help to them in dealing with a terrorist who aimed to kill the maximum number of people in the shortest possible time.

However, Delta was a large group prepared through training and function, and the group of 26 men did not disintegrate, even if their reduced capacity to interpret the information about the rally point might have been partly due to the initial separation of the first units on their way from Oslo to Utøya.

No doubt, the extreme context of Oslo and Utøya on 22 July 2011 must have been highly stressful and threatening even for a highly trained group such as Delta. The situation certainly created moral dilemmas and decision-making problems. At the new rally point, Delta discovered that the boat resources were far too small in relation to the large group of 26, so the officers were faced with a dilemma. If they were to realize the consequences of their choice by rallying far from where they needed to be, in addition to the fact that one of the boats they had access to could only carry a group of six men with full equipment, it would mean that six men would 'go to war', while 20 would be left waiting on the quay in the hope of crossing later. Increased stress levels would have increased the group's cohesion and disabled a splitting of the group. The group members had to stick together to manage the stress and make sense of why they were there. Either they would wait for more boats, or as many as possible of the group members had to board the same boat.

When they overloaded the boat it was not a rational act, but it was likely guided by the ongoing group dynamics and first learned responses. Delta embarked on a crossing that was more dangerous than the immediate threat they were facing from the perpetrator on Utøya. However, at least they were facing the danger together. When they climbed into the small rubber boat, they were in war mode. It was 'one for all and all for one', as if they were prepared to die for each other, as soldiers. Minutes later, the boat was sinking.

Note

1 The Abilene paradox describes a phenomenon where a group of people collectively decide on a course of action that is counter to what many of the individuals in the group want. No one in the group raises objections because they are afraid their individual opinions run counter to those of the group. The phenomenon manifests itself in socially conforming groups, and is a symptom of poor communication and problems of managing agreement.

References

Dekker, S. (2012). *Just Culture: Balancing Safety and Accountability*. 2nd ed. Farnham, UK: Ashgate Publishing Limited.

Dekker, S., Cilliers, P. & Hofmeyr, J. H. (2011). The complexity of failure: Implications of complexity theory for safety investigations. *Safety Science*, 49(6), pp. 939–945.

Fonseca, J. (1998). *Complexity and Innovation in Organizations*. London: Routledge.

Harvey, J. B. (1974). The Abilene paradox: The management of agreement. *Organizational Dynamics*, 3(1), pp. 63–80.

Janis, I. L. (1982). *Groupthink: Psychological Studies of Policy Decisions and Fiascoes*. 2nd ed. Boston, MA: Wadsworth, Cengage Learning.

Mead, G. H. (1934). *Mind, Self and Society*. Chicago: Chicago University Press.

Perrow, C. (1984). *Normal Accidents: Living With High-Risk Technologies*. New York: Basic Books.

Shannon, C. & Weaver, W. (1949). *The Mathematical Theory of Communication*. Urbana: University of Illinois Press.

Taylor, J. & Van Every, E. J. (2014). *When Organization Fails: Why Authority Matters*. New York: Routledge.

Weick K. E. (1990). The vulnerable system: An analysis of the Tenerife air disaster. *Journal of Management*, 16(3), pp. 571–593.

Whyte, W. H. (1952). Groupthink. *Fortune*, March, pp. 14–117.

Part II
Complexity and Practice

5 Organizational Practices and Leadership

Organizational Practices

In the following chapters, I theorize in more depth the processes of organizational practices and leadership in emergency and crisis management organizations, and further link the discussion to the 22 July case. I will mainly focus on two practices: the bureaucratic and the operational.

Operational practices are at the core of activities of public, private, or non-profit organizations that are designated and assigned to prepare for and respond to crises and emergencies, such as the police, military, fire departments, paramedics, hospital emergency units, and various types of rescue organizations. In the everyday activities of these operational organizations, various kinds of administrative routines are integrated. Such activities, which clearly are different from operational activities, are part of the term *bureaucratic practice*.

Bureaucratic Practice

In classical social theory, bureaucracy is characterized in terms of a clear hierarchy with well-defined rules and regulations of work tasks, and how they should be performed (Weber, 2015). In such theory, administrative procedure is at the centre of attention. People and their various and temporal needs are decentred. Their cases demand rational detachment from the people whom the cases concern. The bureaucracy is supposed to be without any emotional influence, subjective convictions, partisanship, or politics with respect to decision-making. It is thus thought of as *independent* not only of the people who inhabit the reality of the administered cases, but also of the administrative professional staff dealing with the cases.

Equal treatment under the law, strong regulatory management, and clear limitations of responsibilities are bureaucratic ideals. Documented facts are seen as the most valid knowledge. The fluctuating and unreliable ways of human beings must not govern and decide their cases, but rather the belief in pure objectivity of the rules themselves. This idea of professional objectivity is based on ideals taken from the natural sciences as well as juridical practice.

Associated with the idea of bureaucracy is the idea of instrumental rationality – a belief that society, institutions, and organizations can be governed and controlled hierarchically and mechanically as if they were machines (Mintzberg, 1980).

The emergence of a bureaucratic understanding of organizations and social institutions has brought forward the idea that it is necessary and possible to separate organizational structure from humans and their cultures. It leads to a practice where politicians and bureaucrats decide the organizational structures of public services and then what culture to develop within that structure.

Much critique has been raised against bureaucratic organization. Weber realized that the bureaucracy had been useful for the establishment of the modern technological society and rule of law, but he was sceptical about the way bureaucracy's invasion of society was constraining human spirit and endeavour. Bureaucracy had contributed to the structuration and systematic administration of society, but at the same time it represented an alienation and threat to diverse, creative, and self-directed human beings.

Crozier (1971) criticized the bureaucracy partly because of the static and meaningless tasks it created for employees and citizens, and partly because it only fitted within stable and predictable environments. According to critics, this makes the bureaucracy unsuitable in a dynamic society and/or when planned changes are to be carried out (Merton, 1957). Although bureaucratic practice has a stabilizing effect on organizations and societies, it also tends to constrain human creativity and make people dependent on routine and predictable activities, which are simple to expand and spread, and very difficult to reduce or remove. Despite the critique, bureaucratic practice has become a very important and increasing part of the activities of professional public service organizations in general, as well as those that deal with crises and emergencies, including the police and the military.

Operational practice

Operational practice stands in contrast to bureaucratic practice, even though it too follows ideas about clear hierarchies, command structures, and responsibilities, whereby leaders at different hierarchical levels are supposed to perform different tasks.

The objective of professional public services is to offer good-quality help for people who are in direct contact with the professionals who perform the services. For the professionals, this means that both rules and budgets have to be bent to get the necessary job done. For the bureaucrat, the converse applies: the rules and budgets come first, and the services have to be adjusted accordingly. Power tensions arise between bureaucrats and the operational professionals due to these different dominating ideas in the two practices.

Such tensions are often found not only between bureaucratic and operational practices, but also within the same practice, such as between leaders and professionals (Johannessen, 2015).

Bureaucratic and Operational Leadership

The two practices imply two different understandings of leadership. *Bureaucratic leadership* is associated with an instrumental and rational way of thinking. Within its language, bureaucratic leadership is spoken of in terms of governance and administration. The idea is that organizations are controllable top-down as closed systems of rules and regulations. By contrast, *operational leadership* is associated with a group-based and mission-based practice.

The idea of the leader as administrator (Fayol, 1916) is part of the origins of bureaucratic practice, whereas leadership as a group effort (Follett, 1926) is associated with the operational practice. Administration and leadership, therefore, can be seen as *opposite* social and organizational practices, the former aiming at stability and discipline, the latter at change.

Leaders are individuals who invite others (the group, organization, or society) to be led into unknown territory, into a reality where it is possible to exist and influence opportunities under conditions of uncertainty and unpredictability. Leaders can only contribute to the social phenomenon of leadership if those 'others' accept their initiative.

However, in many cases, especially in situations of uncertainty, leaders and employees demand administration and rules. They seek stability, safety, and certainty, sustaining what is established while performing repetitive, routine work. Contrary to administration, leadership is concerned with coordination of the members of a group in dynamic and unpredictable situations. Organizations that are preparing for situations of crisis and emergency are most in need of leadership, while their preparations need administration. During crisis, a paradox emerges as the two opposites of administration and leadership become more saliently in tension with each other. The paradox is transformed into a question of judgement: when should we follow the rules and when should we break them?

The operational leader must be able to contribute to this paradoxical practice, that of being similar and different to those who belong to the leader's group. A leader can suggest or insist on openness and variation, and thereby push or lead a group towards more complex and diverse spaces of interaction. However, by doing so the leader might leave a group vulnerable to organizational stress, which will create the need to diminish the spaces of interaction and increase the cohesion of the group.

Operational leaders might want to reduce the paradoxical practices by prioritizing one particular direction of the practice. They might emphasize inspirational and motivational activities associated with performance ideologies, or they may become overly occupied with administration, regulatory constraints, and paralyzing norm governance.

Both directions would tend to dissipate and weaken a leadership practice, consequently undermining the flexible coordination of groups that is needed in an operational practice. It is important for leaders to keep the group and the paradoxes alive by holding spaces of conversation open with respect to the logics of bureaucratic and operational practices.

The phenomenon of leadership emerges in groups as acts of communication. In these acts of communication, leadership practice involves the transformation of ideals into everyday conflicting actions for individuals, who in different ways are bound to and dependent on a group. In general, leadership is therefore a *communicative and ethical practice*.

Leadership as Communicative Practice

People's ability to communicate makes it possible for advanced organizations to operate. Nevertheless, the experiences of organized activity are often neglected and minimized at the expense of a belief in rational and abstract control programmes. At the core of all organizational activity, however, there is a relational and communicative quality between people (Taylor et al., 1996).

Attempts to simplify the relationship between concrete experienced reality and abstract ideals, which is what plans and procedures do, are attempts to simplify ways of relating and communicating between people. In dominating ideas about leadership, the notion exists that some actors, particularly powerful leaders, can position themselves as separate from their organization. They are supposed to see all processes and cause-effect links from an imaginary position 'outside' the processes, and they can even control the activity through rational decisions, procedures, and routines. Communication is in this way of thinking understood as a type of technical procedure with senders and receivers whereby the receivers understand what is said, written, and intended by the sender, in the same way as the sender meant it (Shannon & Weaver, 1949).

However, common experience tells us that decisions taken by powerful leaders are unpredictable, have diffuse consequences, and will be understood and interpreted very differently, particularly when decisions are detached and not communicated or explained directly in context. There are no recognizable boundaries as to where and how decisions might influence the total development of interactions between people in organizations.

When organizational practices form in such dynamic and uncertain ways, there will be strong limitations to leaders' possibilities to extend their control to complex organizational activities. Ultimately, leaders will have no other choice but to move into an open and unknown future and engage in the relations and power games that are played out in their practice.

Leadership as Ethical Practice

Leaders take their initiatives and react, respond, and make choices according to what is going on in their group. They do this through a combination of *judgement and spontaneity*. However, the fact that people make choices does not mean that their behaviour is chosen. Behaviour is a social practice whereby people express themselves from learned assumptions and expectations created in earlier experience with other people's behaviour in similar situations. At the same time, people respond spontaneously and emotionally to what they experience in the present, leading to an evolving situation in which people act and talk in largely unpredictable ways with respect to conversational themes, even though the situations often evolve in ways that are recognizable to the actors involved.

In this highly fluctuating social reality, many buy into the rhetoric that leaders have to be proactive and predict the future: they must be active before a situation arises. Leaders are not only supposed to *adapt* to a situation, but also *prevent* a situation that does not yet exist and about which they cannot know anything.

Although everyday experience tells us that people can sense something is 'brewing' and from that spontaneously and intentionally act on the basis of hunches and assumptions, the result of actions and the evolving of situations in relation to other people's responses will nevertheless be just as unpredictable in those cases as if the actions were not done in a so-called proactive way.

Do Leaders Lead Organizations?

In all organizations, practices exist in which legitimate and illegitimate themes of conversation are communicated. The legitimate themes belong to the organization's public sphere, whereas the illegitimate themes arise in the shadow organization, which is the organized context that is not visible on the organizational charts (Stacey, Griffin & Shaw, 2000). The shadow organization exists in trusted and confidential conversations. The conversational themes emerge in the daily interactions and can thus shift and vary with respect to legitimacy, quality, and potential for support, undermining, or novelty in relation to the legitimate themes.

In organizations where there are strong hierarchies and clear role differences, such as the police and the military, it is difficult for leaders higher up in the hierarchy to come into contact with the shadow themes because those who are in the lower parts of the hierarchy might interpret leader participation in the lower ranks as a form of control. However, in an organization of trust and smaller power differences people could likely interpret a leader's contact with people at all hierarchical levels in the organization as a gesture of involvement and empowerment. No matter what their intentions are, leaders cannot in any case control the shadow organization because its function and purpose is to parallel and, if necessary, undermine the formal organization's hierarchical management control.

If leaders attempt to control the shadow themes, then the themes will likely go underground and soon emerge elsewhere, in arenas where leaders are excluded. A leader might gain trust if he or she tries to convey the differences and conflicts between the legitimate and shadow organization as part of a process to develop mutual understanding of responsibilities between leaders and other employees (Groot, 2009). Nevertheless, acceptance of wider spaces and more openness around shadow themes does not guarantee that new shadow themes will not emerge in other arenas.

Change in organizations is linked to the terms by which the shadow themes are brought into contact with the legitimate themes and the legitimate organization. The gap between the legitimate and illegitimate themes means that leaders have limited power to control and change organizations. Leaders are often surprised by how their decisions about strategies and objectives in organizations end up different from their initial intentions.

Hence, an organization cannot be properly understood as a controllable hierarchical organized system or structure designed by leaders, within which people act. According to complexity theory (Stacey, 2010), organizations can rather be understood as self-organizing processes created by themes of communication that are coordinated and patterned between people. Even if some leaders are authorized to influence themes of communication more strongly than other individuals do, this does not mean that the organization is controlled by powerful leaders or a system outside interacting people, because the themes of communication sustain, move, and change the organization in unpredictable ways.

Sustaining and changing authority and identity are phenomena of organization that emerge in communication (Taylor & Van Every, 2014), in the sense that the importance of themes of conversation in an organization is not evenly distributed among people. Since organizations are not controlled by anyone alone, the idea that leaders are leading organizations becomes problematic. Organizations cannot be objects of leadership, but by influencing themes of communication acts of leadership can be performed.

As shown in the discussion so far, my thesis is that organizational and leadership practices can be analysed and understood in terms of *communication*, *power*, *identity*, and *ethics*. In the following, I further theorize that the importance and priority of these phenomena differ in the different practices, and that the meaning of *organization* depends on how these phenomena are understood.

References

Crozier, M. (1971). *The World of the Office-Worker*. Chicago: University of Chicago Press.

Fayol, H. (1916/1949). *General and Industrial Management*. London: Pitman.

Follett, M. P. (1926). The giving of orders. In: H. C. Metcalf (ed.). *Scientific Foundations of Business Administration*. Baltimore, MD: Williams & Wilkins, pp. 29–37.

Groot, N. (2009). Senior executives and the emergence of local responsibilities: A complexity approach to identity development and performance improvement. *International Journal of Learning and Change*, 3(3), pp. 264–280.

Johannessen, S. O. (2015). Reforming the Norwegian police: Cultural change as a restoration of organizational ideologies, myths and practices. *Nordisk Politiforskning*, 2(2), pp. 167–182.

Merton, R. K. (1957). *Social Theory and Social Structure*. Glencoe, IL: Free Press, pp. 195–206.

Mintzberg, H. (1980). Structure in 5's: A synthesis of the research on organization design. *Management Science*, 26(3), pp. 322–341.

Shannon, C. & Weaver, W. (1949). *The Mathematical Theory of Communication*. Urbana: University of Illinois Press.

Stacey, R. D. (2010). *Complexity and Organizational Reality*. London: Routledge.

Stacey, R. D., Griffin, D. & Shaw, P. (2000). *Complexity and Management: Fad or Radical Challenge to Systems Thinking?* London: Routledge.

Taylor, J. R., Cooren, F., Giroux, N. & Robichaud, D. (1996). The communicational basis of organization: Between the conversation and the text. *Communication Theory*, 6, pp. 1–39.

Taylor, J. & Van Every, E. J. (2014). *When Organization Fails: Why Authority Matters*. New York: Routledge.

Weber, M. (2015). Bureaucracy. In: T. Waters & D. Waters (ed. and trans.). *Weber's Rationalism and Modern Society*. New York: Palgrave MacMillan, pp. 73–127.

6   Communication

Communication as Organization

Organizational communication researchers Taylor & Van Every (2000) hold that organizations are constituted by communication. In explaining how organization and coordination can happen, they link communication to *authority* (Taylor & Van Every, 2014). They see authority as a property of communication, and hence of organization in practice (ibid, p. xx). They refer to Barley (1996, p. 3), who claims that the basis of authority is either hierarchical office (position) or skilled practice (expertise), and that there must be a congruence of position and expertise if authority is to be effective.

In Barley's argument, the communities of practice representing expert authority form the basis of coordination. This coordination does not follow 'vertical' position but is more 'horizontal', which in Barley's view implicates that organizations must find forms of organizing that are more horizontal instead of the vertical hierarchies that have traditionally been preferred as organizational structures. Barley's call coincides with widespread calls since the 1980s for horizontal organizing and shifts towards more group-oriented and team-oriented organizational forms (Johannessen, 2009). However, the vertical hierarchy still persists to a large extent as the preferred way of preserving and enforcing organizations, not least in the police and the military.

Barley seems to suggest that there are two rather static sources of authority in organizations: experts and positions. This might fit with the two organizational practices: bureaucratic (position) and operational (experts). However, there is a risk of oversimplifying when an organizational phenomenon such as authority is constrained to those two dimensions, because we must be able to analyse authority as an aspect of the *dynamics* within and between the organizational practices, i.e. in terms of processes of communication, power, identity, and ethics.

Taylor & Van Every (2014) argue that, despite the decoupling of position and expertise through sustained hierarchical layers of management, organizations can function because middle management buffers senior managers' loss of hierarchical authority by translating abstract strategies into concrete operational practices, sometimes without any noticeable changes for the operational practitioners. They go on to hypothesize that experts and positions are agents of organizations who 'feel authorised to speak for it, to act in its name and enunciate its purposes' (Taylor & Van Every, 2014, p. 5). They focus on:

> the constitutive role that communication plays in generating the system of authority that holds the organization together . . . [and it is by] looking at the organization as constructed in and by communication that we can better understand the complexity of the authority issues that are at stake, and why they sometimes lead to breakdown.
>
> (Taylor & Van Every, 2014, pp. 5–6)

They are making the point that between experts and positions communication holds the conflicts and relations of authority together in an organization, so if the organization breaks down, it will be because communication and authority relations have broken down. Similarly, as seen in the 22 July case, I maintain that organization dissolved because communications within and between the groups of bureaucratic and operational practitioners broke down.

During a crisis, we might well have a situation in which layers of management that normally function detached from each other become exposed and vulnerable, as they suddenly find themselves dependent on each other. Relations are stripped bare when a crisis of authority emerges. As authority relations collapse and suffer from lack of clarity and as critical functional areas are abandoned, organizational coordination will collapse and people will be left increasingly helpless and incompetent. This occurred in the 22 July case when the senior leaders left open a vacuum of operational leadership where they were supposed to coordinate the response to a national emergency.

Communication in the Two Practices

One way of distinguishing between organizational practices, albeit the basis of authority is by identifying the ways in which knowledge is created and used, as well as what types of knowledge are valued most. In bureaucratic practices, knowledge is valued in the form of abstract facts, laws, rules, and regulations in written form, whereas in operational practices, knowledge is valued as concrete ways of solving practical problems – a knowledge acquired and enacted in oral form and shared in the operational community.

Communities of practice (Wenger, 1998) are recognizable by language and knowledge, which are sustained over time and are characterized by consistent habits. According to Taylor & Van Every (2014), communities of practice rely on the attribution of authority to do their work. Because each community of practice becomes a source of authority for its members, the resulting transactional arrangements and understandings will lead to organizational heterogeneity that will give rise to conflicts, as I have explained earlier in the case of bureaucratic and operational practices in emergency organizations.

However, for Taylor & Van Every (2014, p. 7) 'Organization starts from practice', i.e. organization comes after practice. What they call practice is linked to skills of experts in performing activity: 'It is the experts' skill that explains their authority because they are the ones who author the organization, in the concrete, by the contribution they (and thereby it) make to society at large' (ibid, p. 7). This seems limited to what I have called *operational practice*. Taylor and Van Every see operational practitioners as socialized into groups, in which they operate not so much in a formal hierarchy as they do in the group. Interactions in the group are then the source of expert authority.

It is much less clear how Taylor and Van Every see the community of bureaucratic practitioners. Moreover, if we are to see authority as a fundamental phenomenon of organization, it is equally unclear what their general view is on authority in relation to *social cohesion*.

Philosopher Bertrand Russell (1949) saw authority as a mechanism of social cohesion, a necessary external force by which a group of some size is coordinated. For him, authority was the same as hierarchy or position. This seems to be what Taylor and Van Every refer to as organization, which is the idea that organization exists as:

> a 'person' whose purposes must be enunciated and then translated into the language of members' practice, if they are to be its agents. It is the intervening 'authorization' of the organization's purposes, at least as the managers see it, that legitimates their role in the positions. They feel entitled to act as agents because they claim to embody its authority in their words: as its spokespersons. They see themselves as the translators.
>
> (Taylor & Van Every, 2014, p. 7)

I argue that when managers operate and think in this way, it is too a practice – a bureaucratic practice.

Peirce and Mead

Drawing on the work of Charles Sanders Peirce (1955), Taylor & Van Every (2014, p. 7) hold that there are:

> three components of purposeful activity: an actor (a first), and acted on (a second) and a third, or that which interprets and justifies what is happening, gives it meaning, and supplies as script that actors can follow. The result is a practice and a community that embodies it in their work and collective understandings of what they are doing and why they do it.

Taylor & Van Every (2014, p. 9) go on to state that the third ('Thirdness') is made present in the everyday conversations of community members by references made in the third person or to another embodiment of authority, such as 'company policy' or 'management'. Furthermore:

> It is the transactions that organize. But it is also disagreements and disputes over the transactional 'law' of the relationship, and the resulting difficulties of establishing who is obliged to do what for whom, that lead to a breakdown of normal relating and a crisis of authority . . .
> . . . The question arises of what happens when the material object that links the two parties is in rapid evolution – has changed in value, perhaps even dramatically – while the transaction, and the beneficiary's perception of the object, has not. Our answer must be that any radical change in the object implies a renegotiation of the relationship. Otherwise, incoherence will be created.

What do Taylor and Van Every mean by object and embodiment of authority? They are clearly talking not only of physical objects, but also of objects that have to do with relationships, i.e. social structure. Furthermore, they seem to suggest that authority has something to do with imaginary structures/objects or patterns of action created by human relations, like when people talk about 'the system' or 'the organization':

> The concept of thirdness is defined in two distinct but interrelated ways. First, thirdness is a body of understanding about an object . . . Second, thirdness is a set of understandings of a transactional relationship, in dealing with an object . . . Thirdness, in this second sense, is a convention to which members subscribe and that carries its own authority.
> (ibid, p. 9)

If we turn to Mead, a different light might be shed on our understanding of the communicative nature of organization and authority.

Social Acts and the Generalized Other

Mead suggested that communicative interaction between humans takes the form of a *social act* (Stacey, 2010, p. 145). A process of communicative interaction can be seen as involving interpretation (i.e. ascertaining the meaning of the actions or remarks of the other person) and definition, which indicates to another person how he or she should act (Blumer, 1969). As there can be no absolute prediction of the particular response of the other person, this dual process of definition and interpretation creates both mutual understanding and misunderstandings, and thus operates both to sustain established patterns of joint conduct and to open them up to transformation.

Humans have evolved a capacity to interpret, understand, and adopt the attitude of another person; 'attitude' means a person's tendency to act. When acting, each individual takes the concrete attitudes of others whom they are observing or experiencing directly and at the same time the individual also takes the abstract attitude of what Mead called '*the generalized other*', which is the attitude of a group, organization, or the society in which they live (Stacey, 2010, p. 148).

Self-consciousness

In the course of human history, individuals became aware of themselves as objects in the eyes of others – a relationship between 'me' and 'I'. In the words of Stacey (2010, p. 148): 'A self, as a relationship between "me" and "I", has therefore emerged, as well as an awareness of that self, that is, self-consciousness'. The evolution of self-consciousness, however, not only involves a person becoming self-aware in terms of experiencing the existence of one's own physical body in the world, but also in terms of experiencing the importance of relations to others for the process of discovering one's own existence. One needs to discover others in order to discover oneself. Mead referred to this paradoxical experience as the simultaneous emergence of mind, self, and society as a process of human interaction (Mead, 1934).

Social Objects

Social acts involve the cooperation of many people, in which the different parts of the act undertaken by different individuals appear in the act of each individual. The tendency to act as others act is present in the conduct of each individual involved and this presence is responsible for the appearance of what Mead (1938) called *the social object* in the experience of each individual. This is the basis of *coordination* and hence of *organization*.

The social object is a generalization that is particularized by members of a group or society in their immediate actions. Hence, social objects are not physical objects, but experiences of social structure constructed as a result of social interaction. However, in that experience, social objects can be reified as physical objects, for example when people talk about organized patterns as 'the system'.

Physical Objects as Patterns of Social Acting

On the other hand, physical objects, such as technologies, are also social objects (Johannessen & Stacey, 2005). Technologies are patterns in social acting that take on meaning as we use them and talk about them. They are simultaneous *generalizing and particularizing processes*. In their communicative acts, people construct generalized meanings of technological artefacts. In the particularization process, the meaning of this reality can change. A car can be seen and used as a means of transport by most, but a bomb by some. The existence of physical objects, such as tools and generalized techniques for using them, thus creates generalized tendencies for large numbers of people to act in similar ways in similar situations. However, in their particularization, these generalized tendencies may change.

Social Structure as Self-organizing Social Processes

Social structure cannot exist before it is created, and it is created in the very same communicative interaction processes that provide meaning to it, as an 'it'. Hence, meaning and structure emerge at the same time. Structure and process not only mutually influence each other but they both emerge at the same time in social interaction. Objects are both structure and process. Since physical structures do not exist for us before they are given meaning, and since meaning emerges in human interaction, any physical objects involved in such interactions will necessarily become social objects.

When experiencing social structure, such as an organization, people tend to reify and construct images of a physical object, such as a machine or an organism (Morgan, 1997). When experiencing a physical object, people 'process' it into a social object: a socially constructed meaning of a pattern of behaviour. This simultaneous construction of physical objects as social objects is the experience of emergent self-organizing social processes (Johannessen & Stacey, 2005). This formulation is different from the one provided by Taylor and Van Every when they talk about 'thirdness', but clearly has something in common with it.

Organization, Coordination, and Authority

Similar to Mead, the insight provided by Taylor and Van Every (inspired by Peirce) is that the relationship following from meaning emerging in communication is the basis of coordination, which is organization. Taylor and Van Every link this coordination to authority, and thus indicate that authority is the emergence of meaning between people.

However, in contrast to Mead, their discussion lacks an elaborate explanation of this process. In particular, this concerns Mead's idea that people must be able to take the attitude of *the generalized other* to themselves in order to perform coordinated actions. The generalized other is obviously a construction of the mind: the attitude of the group towards oneself cannot be real in the sense that a person is able to know what attitude everybody in a group takes to the person. However, the capacity of the individual to take the attitude of the group is sufficient for different persons to be able to adapt so that they seem coordinated in similar situations in a large group, such as an organization or a society.

Taylor and Van Every appear to argue that this coordinating phenomenon of the large group is authority, and that it flows from people having similar interpretations of what they call 'thirdness', which is an imagined or constructed feeling of 'something' driving or scripting people's actions within certain limits. I argue that this 'force of thirdness' is the same as what Mead referred to as the generalized other, which is the imaginary group/ organization/society acting as if it were a person. It follows from this that authority is the same as the attitude taken by the individual towards the self as a felt attitude taken by the generalized other/the group towards the individual.

In linking Mead more closely to Taylor and Van Every, I suggest that the slightly mysterious thirdness is produced in interaction and is experienced by the individual as an attitude towards the self. It is the individual 'I' that 'forces' or persuades the individual 'me' – the self – to act in such a particular way that the individual 'I' thinks is acceptable for the group. In this way, we can link agency to Taylor and Van Every's idea that authority and organization emerge in communication, which is what makes the individual 'I' act in relation to or on behalf of another person, group, or organization, 'They'. Agency is the basis for individual action, but agency is dependent on social interaction and the emergence of meaning and/or authority.

Taylor & Van Every (2014, p. 13) also refers to Greimas (1993), who saw the organization as 'an initiator and source of all authority'. This looks like the very same idea of organization as described by Bertrand Russell (1949) in *Authority and the Individual*. Authority has something to do with how individuals sense an impact of government, organizations, institutions, and society, which in Mead's terms would be the sensing of the generalized other towards the self.

Compared with Peirce, Greimas seemed to take an even more mechanistic view when he talked about 'sender' and 'sender-to'. He splits the relationships between persons very clearly, as well as the relationship between the person and the organization. The idea of the person and the system is widespread. In his reading of Mead, Stacey rejects this idea and argues that there is no reality in the organization as a system, other than the possibility of thinking about the organization *as if* it were a system or a thing in the sense of a social object (Stacey, 2010).

The idea of the organization as a system personifies the organization and hence the way it performs actions on the individual. Whether one thinks of the organization as an organism or a mechanical thing makes no difference to this basic notion that the organization contains power or can impact the individual in such a way that the individual will have to submit to it. It seems to me that it is this way of seeing power that is referred to as authority by Taylor and Van Every.

In Stacey's interpretation of Mead's thought, there is no clear splitting between the individual and other individuals, groups, organizations, or societies. A splitting, in the sense of individual uniqueness, is the expression of a paradox. Persons become persons because they are social, and groups become groups because individuals interact. A person is both an individual and not an individual. Based on Mead, Stacey explains how this paradoxical process can come about by the phenomenon of emergence in social interaction.

In social interaction, something different emerges in the experience of the persons than what is physically and rationally visible to those persons as individuals in the first place. A *sense* of the group or organization or society (i.e. of the generalized other) *emerges* in the individual as a result of the emergence of meaning in conversations, which is communicating in the medium of significant symbols (i.e. language). The sense of the group cannot be seen or heard; it cannot be pointed to, and as such it does not exist in the world. It only exists in the constructed world of the person's social mind. That is why Mead argued that mind, self, and society are different aspects of the same process, a process of interaction and emergence (Mead, 1934). This resonates with ideas from complexity theory about interaction and emergence. Hence, the foundation is there for a social and organizational theory of complexity (Johannessen & Kuhn, 2012, Volume I).

Authority as Experience of Organization

I think there are both similarities and differences between Stacey and the co-authors Taylor and Van Every and their sources of inspiration. The similarities are their insistence that organizations are communicative interactions in which coordinated actions emerge in the interactions. One of the differences is that Taylor and Van Every hold onto the splitting of the organization and the individual, and treat authority as a constructive force of the organization.

Stacey treats the coordinating phenomenon of organization as the capacity of humans to take the attitude of the group to themselves. Agency, therefore, is an individual phenomenon emerging in social interaction. Organizations do not possess agency, but when the sense of the organization emerges in social interaction, this leads to the feeling of expansion of identity. The sense of personal identity becomes threatened by this larger and more powerful group identity. However, a person also senses that as an individual more can be accomplished when this experience of organization emerges than when it is not felt. The experience of enlarged identity drives a person *to identify with* and act on behalf of the fantasy of the group/organization. It is not the organization or group that acts as if it was an individual. It is authority as basis for individual action that is identical to an individual's experience of organization.

We turn now to see some excerpts of how communication and authority emerged in the interactions between groups during the police operation on 22 July 2011.

Communication in the Police Operation

In the 22 July case, the tightly coupled Delta members and the loosely coupled NBPD groups and operations centre could have enhanced their chances of succeeding more quickly if they had coupled their communication more tightly. By decoupling, the two groups prolonged the time of confusion.

When structure and meaning were lost for members of the police groups on 22 July, many tried to regain the structure, although much of the time they were only concerned for themselves and not for other groups. This led to loss of coordination. When the Delta units did not receive clear confirmation about the rally point from the NBPD, they did not spend more energy on coordination with the NBPD's operations centre, even though this relationship was crucial to the speed and quality of the operation. Instead, they centred their attention on their own group's coordination.

However, Delta was dependent on the NBPD, and vice versa. Interdependency leads to problems in organized networks if people forget how their own efforts to tighten the organizing of their local group can lead to loss of organization and coordination both within and in relation to other groups in the network. As these organizing and 'de-organizing' effects ripple across interdependent networks, the effects are not linear. Minor coordination problems at one place in a network can escalate non-linearly to become large problems elsewhere in the network.

Communication technologies can dampen these effects by fast coordination functions. However, during a crisis, the enormous gain from successful communication through technology can be underestimated if it ceases too rapidly due to temporal technological problems. Delta might have gained from dedicating a minute to clarifying communication with the NBPD's operations centre and with the Oslo PD's operational staff. However, a more important fact is that Delta had its separate command structure in Oslo called Delta KO. It was Delta KO that initiated the order to head for Utøya.

Delta KO was in charge of providing information to the Delta units, making an initial operational plan, and coordinating with other groups and units, including the NBPD operations centre. The time horizon for this coordination was the 30 minutes before Delta came into the district of North Buskerud.

Although Delta KO as well as the Oslo PD's operational staff had access to Google Maps, on which crossings to Utøya and boat marinas were clearly visible, this crucial information was never communicated to the Delta units. There is nothing to suggest that Delta KO needed help, because there was no request to Oslo PD's operational staff to help with information collection about the Utøya area. The 22 July Commission Report says nothing about this crucial loss of coordination. To date there are no consistent answers about this from the people involved other than some suggesting that they thought Delta had no need for information because the assumption was that the units would coordinate when they reached NBPD.

Weick comments: 'nonstop talk . . . is a crucial source of coordination in complex systems that are susceptible to catastrophic disasters' (2001, p. 115). According to Delta, not only was there little or no communication between Delta KO and the Delta units, but there was little communication *between* the Delta units and even *within* each Delta unit during the 30 – minute car ride from Oslo to the mainland opposite Utøya. Delta members might have been individually preparing for the task ahead, but too little communication within and between the groups could have left them less organized and coordinated, and eventually less prepared and more dependent on NBPD when they arrived near Utøya mainland quay.

As a result, Delta ended up in confusion about basic matters such as the rally point, crossing point, and boat resources. This might have been due to them being too quick to designate ongoing talk as low priority. However, lack of coordinating talk was a major weakness in general during the three-hour police operation on 22 July 2011. Together with the loose coupling within the NBPD and between the NBPD and Delta, this made the operation vulnerable to disruptions.

Research has suggested that panic will erupt when members of groups lack goals that transcend the self-interests of each participant (Bass, 1990). This difference existed between Delta and the ordinary police officers. Delta was aiming at solving the situation as a group while the NBPD police disrupted already from the point where emergency calls overflowed the NBPD operations centre. One operator was left at the operation centre. She focused mainly on taking emergency calls from Utøya and left uncoordinated the police operation that could stop the ongoing event. While the two officers that were most trained to handle a terrorist took the rubber boat in which they later picked up Delta, the two officers that were least trained for armed response went to the mainland quay as first responders.

Division of labour was the centre of attention, but divisions of labour work best when the task is simple, predictable, trained, and not stressful. The division of labour at NBPD was none of this. It seemed more or less random. Splitting the organization at random under conditions of stress would have reinforced the stress. Hence, the communication between the various people was fragmented and coordination was lost in time and space. Everyone had to make sense of the drama alone or in very small groups. When people scattered, the need for precise coordinated communication *increased*, yet the operations centre's ability to do this *decreased* and eventually it crumbled under the pressure. In the event, there was no leadership to coordinate the collapsing organization.

Weick (2001, p. 118) refers to Eisenberg's (1990) term *non-disclosive intimacy* to describe group action that favours coordination over thinking alike, mutual respect over agreement, trust over empathy, diversity over homogeneity, loose coupling over tight coupling, and strategic communication over unrestricted candour. Non-disclosive intimacy works best in stable environments when the task is predictable. Tightly coupled groups are best suited for situations that are unstable and unpredictable.

Delta is a tightly coupled police group and more so than any other police group. It tends to lean towards a more balanced group action of thinking alike *and* coordination, of agreement *and* mutual respect, and of trust *and* empathy. However, when it comes to the other aspects, Delta tends to favour tight coupling over loose coupling, homogeneity over diversity, and under certain norms unrestricted candour over strategic communication, as might be expected from such a group.

Delta is a group of men who are trained (and thus overlearned) in exactly the same way and for much of the time they keep themselves separated from other police units. Unrestricted candour is tolerated, but only during certain group meetings and discussions outside operations, never during an operation. After open discussion, the chief's decision is final and must not be discussed further. However, Delta units are also trained to have a high degree of group autonomy. They have adopted the military leadership idea of acting according to the intention of the commander without having to receive instructive orders. This might explain why Delta KO did not provide the Delta units with crucial information about the Utøya area. Once the mission was set by the general operational objective, which in the 22 July case was to stop the shooter(s) at Utøya, the units with their assigned action leader then had to coordinate and solve the mission on their own.

The problem was that they were not alone; they were either dependent or made themselves dependent on others when they came to the mainland area opposite Utøya. When they discovered they were dependent on the 'fragmented others', this caused confusion in their group as well as more fragmentation in relation to the others.

Cohesion and Fragmentation

However, the pattern of fragmentation was widespread. Within the groups of senior police leaders of the Oslo PD, within the POD, and between those groups, there were various degrees of couplings, but mostly fragmentation. The police response on 22 July was in general not one of a coordinated force, simply because there was no possibility that everyone could know each other well enough to take a particular and clear role in relation to everyone else in the situation.

When Delta responded to the confusion, it prioritized holding its group together without the necessary openness that could have kept the group from gravitating inwards. The group dynamics tightened and the group started to favour thinking alike and agreement over coordination and trust, while it strengthened homogeneity and tight couplings. The operational objective was to get to Utøya and neutralize the shooter or shooters. It was a group objective and therefore everyone was ready to jump into the same boat.

The only person who had formal authority to prevent the group from overloading the boat was the Delta action leader. He could have stood out from the tightly coupled group and thought of his role in charge of the action as having a slightly reflective distance from the rest of his group. By making individual sense of the situation on behalf of the group, he could have been able to come up with a more sensible solution than to overload the rubber boat.

However, that would mean splitting the group, which risked a loss of authority. By not taking this risk, he exposed the group to another risk: the treacherous and powerful dynamics of groupthink where he as leader became absorbed as 'one for all and all for one'.

In the crucial moments when it was essential that he could be the 'one and only' who stood out as leader to nudge the group out of its hypnotic mode, he was gambling with the authority of the group. It seems that Delta had not trained him or any of their leaders for such a moment.

Weick (2001, p. 118) states: 'Closer ties permit clearer thinking, which enables people to find paths around obstacles'. In the case of Delta, closer ties might have *prevented* clearer thinking and meant they were *unable* to find paths around obstacles such as the limitation of the boat capacity. More complex situations require a higher degree of complexity in the response pattern.

When the bomb exploded in Oslo, Delta came directly from a training session into a real situation. According to their own statement, they thought about their response when they approached Utøya mainland quay as a response to a hostage situation, which meant that they mobilized their habitual response patterns. It is not clear what exactly they had been training earlier in the day, but it is unlikely that they had acquired any fresh and more complex response patterns that were useful for the challenges they ended up facing, i.e. coordination across a network of fragmented units, unclear hierarchies, and unclear resources. It is most likely they had been training for isolated situations, as they normally do.

Newly acquired, more complex, collective responses are more vulnerable to disruption than habitual overlearned responses (Weick, 2001, p. 130). In Delta's case, many of the organizational challenges in their mission to Utøya were not like anything they ever had experienced before.

When they were being thrown into a real situation that was very different from their learned responses, they very quickly had to create an idea of what was going on. If they thought the situation on Utøya was a hostage situation, then that would be a very different idea to an ongoing mass shooting. Perhaps the idea of a hostage-taker served a different purpose? It would be an idea that would lower their stress levels because they were most comfortable to pursue a hostage situation as a tactical pattern. Perhaps they could believe in their superiority by relating to the set–piece situation of hostage-taking, even if they were relating to an illusion? Perhaps that was what the change of rally point was all about?

By prioritizing a safe and controllable rally point, they could at least have one certain and stable point of reference where they could believe that it made sense to cross to the island to confront a totally confusing, unpredictable, and deadly situation.

References

Barley, S. R. (1996). Technicians in the work place: Ethnographic evidence for bringing work into organization studies. *Administrative Science Quarterly*, 41, pp. 404–440.

Bass, B. M. (1990). *Bass and Stogdill's Handbook of Leadership: Theory, Research and Managerial Applications*. 3rd ed. New York: Free Press.

Blumer, H. (1969). *Symbolic Interactionism. Perspectives and Method*. Los Angeles: University of California Press.

Eisenberg, E. M. (1990). Jamming: Transcendence through organizing. *Communication Research*, 17, pp. 139–164.

Greimas, A. J. (1993). Préface. In: J. Courtés (ed.). *Sémiotique narrative et discursive*. Paris: Hachette, pp. 5–25.

Johannessen, S. O. (2009). The complexity turn in studies of organisations and leadership: Relevance and implications. *International Journal of Learning and Change*, 3(3), pp. 214–229.

Johannessen, S. O. & Kuhn, L. (eds) (2012). *Complexity in Organization Studies, Volume I—IV*. London: Sage.

Johannessen, S. O. & Stacey, R. D. (2005). Technology as social object: A complex responsive processes perspective. In: R. D. Stacey (ed.). *Experiencing Emergence in Organisations: Local Interaction and the Emergence of Global Pattern*. London: Routledge, pp. 142–163.

Mead, G. H. (1934). *Mind, Self and Society*. Chicago: Chicago University Press.

Mead, G. H. (1938). *The Philosophy of the Act*. Chicago: Chicago University Press.

Morgan, G. H. (1997). *Images of Organization*. London: Sage.

Peirce, C. S. (1955/2011). *Philosophical Writings of Peirce*. Selected and Edited by J. Buchler. New York: Dover Publications, Inc.

Russell, B. (1949/1985). *Authority and the Individual*. London: George Allen & Unwin.

Stacey, R. D. (2010). *Complexity and Organizational Reality*. London: Routledge.

Taylor, J. R. & Van Every, E. J. (2000). *The Emergent Organization: Communication as Its Site and Surface*. Mahwah, NJ: Lawrence Erlbaum.

Taylor, J. & Van Every, E. J. (2014). *When Organization Fails: Why Authority Matters*. New York: Routledge.

Wenger, K. E. (1998). *Communities of Practice: Learning, Meaning and Identity*. New York: Cambridge University Press.

Weick, K. E. (2001). *Making Sense of Organization*. Malden, MA: Blackwell.

7 Power, Identity, and Ethics

Power and Identity

Every person is a result of a history and upbringing. To become a person means being influenced and socialized by the political conditions into which the individual has been born and brought up. Power is always present in human practice, in the actions and interactions enacted by humans; it takes the form of recognition, enabling, loyalty, submission, and dominance.

Everyday actions are constrained and enabled by power relations and experiences of identity, which are acts of inclusion and exclusion that define people 'inside' or 'outside' various groups in society or an organization (Elias & Scotson, 1994; Dalal, 1998). This insider/outsider dynamic define the close link between *power and identity* in organizational practices. The existence of one group is dependent on the existence of another group. Organizing is dependent on inclusion and exclusion themes holding different groups (large and small) together and separated from each other.

Ideology and Gossip

According to Dalal (1998), ideology is closely related to power relations between groups. It has to do with what feels for the members of a group natural to do and say in their relations with other groups. Dalal draws on German–British sociologist Norbert Elias, who emphasized the importance of gossip as a communicative mechanism by which power and ideology are sustained between groups (Dalal, 1998, p. 118). Dalal summarizes the typical relationship between ideology and gossip in that the content of the ideology takes the form of dichotomies or binary pairs, where the characteristics of 'them' are negative-laden as opposed to those positive-laden characteristics of 'us'.

Seen from Delta's perspective, 'they' (the NBPD police) were not able to handle a terrorism attack, unlike 'us' (Delta). As the less powerful group, the NBPD police could not have disagreed with that perspective, so they would have taken a *similar* attitude towards themselves as Delta did, and in that way they would have preserved the status quo of the power relation, which is the exact purpose of ideology.

When Delta arrived in the NBPD's area, the operator at the operations centre suddenly left the decision on the rally point to Delta. In that particular moment, the Delta officer did not clarify that he was not in charge. He did not seem to be conscious of the risk that the NBPD in the critical situation would either invert the formal power relation or revert it to the basic ideological expert relation. Without stating it explicitly, the NBPD wanted Delta to take *formal* responsibility based on their everyday *informal* power position, even if this meant turning the formal hierarchy and procedures on their head. The NBPD's notion was that the Delta members were dominant, they were the experts, and they had to lead. *Both* groups reverted to this basic ideological notion of authority.

When the Delta officer in unit D35 did not explicitly refuse to take charge by turning down the NBPD's surrender of power, the NBPD was drawn into the habitual pattern, which was the basic assumption of the relation between Delta and normal police. The operator interpreted the Delta officer's question about the rally point as an order. The Delta officer, who was also caught in the same ideological power pattern, took the lack of confirmation to mean either confirmation or confusion.

Either way, it confirmed to him the ideological assumption that the local police were unreliable and Delta was the powerful unit that had to proceed according to its own decisions and judgement of the situation. This took them to Elstangen. Later, when criticism was raised about this move, Delta pointed at the least powerful. It was the NBPD's responsibility, and if the decision was a mistake, it was NBPD's mistake.

Dalal (1998, p. 118) states: 'charisma is attributed to the more powerful "us" and stigma to the less powerful "them"'. Referring to Elias & Scotson's (1994) study of the power relations between 'the established and the outsiders', Dalal further says: 'The gossip streams were full of praise gossip concerning the established, and blame gossip concerning the outsiders' (Dalal, 1998, p. 89). Not unlike the relationship between Delta and NBPD.

Acts of Inclusion and Exclusion: Insiders and Outsiders

Organizations are intersubjective worlds. In ongoing processes, it becomes difficult for all participants to pinpoint what comes first in these processes – the individual or 'the others' (i.e. the group, organization, society) – since the individual and the group are created simultaneously as one and the same emerging phenomenon – *the social individual* (Elias, 1991).

Although the employees of emergency organizations are involved in activities across different practices, for most people one practice dominates their own activities and is thus experienced as an *insider activity*. Others' activities then become *outsider activities*. When activities in different widespread practices interact, conflict arises precisely because people who perform these different practices experience power and identity issues associated with their dominating insider activity in relation to others, who are enacting outsider activity. Conflicts may become strong and amplified if people in different practices feel that it is 'natural' that other practices should submit to what is considered the dominating practice and dominating ideology (Dalal, 1998).

Conflicting organizational practices cannot be removed without rendering the organization dysfunctional. The conflicting views are a necessary precursor and consequence for meaningful practices to exist in organizations. Although conflicts may be locked into patterns of relating that prevent something new from arising, conflicts may also be the sources of novelty, for instance, in the form of compromises, which brings forth solutions that no one has thought about before. Also, patterns of action that function as 'good enough' can develop as part of compromises, even if the patterns have dysfunctional features.

Organizations as Practices of Inclusion and Exclusion

As I have argued thus far, organizations are ongoing practices that are repeated and potentially changed in conversations and patterns of communicative relating between people employed by and associated with the organizations. If organizations are seen in this way, then there is no reason to separate organizational structures from organizational cultures. Organizational charts and formal structures are also expressions of organizational practices.

In the same way as meaning in an ordinary conversation between people emerges without design, so do organizational practices and the organization emerge without design in communicative activities. Communication cannot have an inside and an outside. This is why organizations seen as organizational practices of communicative relating cannot be understood as bounded by real boundaries – like systems.

However, people are included and excluded in practices and these inclusion and exclusion dynamics are organizing people as organizations. People who are perceived as outside an organization are included and excluded in particular ways in organizational practices, as are those who are perceived as inside the organization. Organizations emerge in such communicative inclusion and exclusion processes.

Ethics

There is a widespread notion that leaders can define values for organizations and that these values generally have a given meaning for everyone when manifested in action. However, action often differ considerably from what is intended in defined values (Taylor, 2005). Some researchers have suggested that people have 'espoused values' and 'real values' (Argyris & Schön, 1978), indicating that people possess two sets of values: one that is permanent, 'real', and kept silent inside the person, and one that is enacted when the person is in the company of other people.

Mead, however, developed a theory of values in which conflict is at the very core (Griffin, 2002, p. 193). He distinguishes between cult values and functional values. Cult values are *idealizations* emerging in the evolution of a society or an organization (Stacey, 2010, p. 164). Such cult values present an image of an idealized future without conflict and constraints, and generate a feeling of enlarged personality in a group, whereby individuals envisage themselves as able to achieve anything.

If cult values are applied directly to practical action by precisely and unequivocally defining that action, without allowing for the kind of variation that is required by every specific situation, those undertaking such action will form a cult in which they exclude all who do not comply with their cult's values, and include those who conform to them. In this way, collective 'we' identities are created for all individuals in both groups. Cult values are therefore closely associated with power. The patterns both enable and constrain the actors at the same time.

Functionalization of Cult Values

When people experience real and conflicting patterns of action as a contrast to the ideal and conflict-free formulations of cult values, they experience what Mead (1923) called *functionalization*. The functionalization of cult values is the enactment of values in the ordinary, everyday relations between people. Humans adapt their behaviour when they meet other humans; they do not have two sets of values. Rather, they have the ability to formulate ideals, which inspires their future action. At the same time, interactions with other people who also are inspired by ideals constrain action and produce conflict (Joas, 2000). Practice, in the sense of functionalizing cult values inevitably leads either to conflict (instability) or to negotiations of compromise around such conflict (stability).

There has long existed a popular formula for success among leaders and consultants to create engagement in visions and on that basis develop common cultures and values for an organization (Ouchi, 1981; Senge, 1990). Leaders voice the kind of culture and values to which it is most noble for employees to adhere. However, adhering to the idealized common values in such formulae is often an expression and demand for one-way thinking and obedience in order to create 'common understanding'. The notion of organizations being driven by common values and visions is not congruent with change, innovative thinking, and challenges to established truths. Moreover, organizations cannot have human qualities such as values and visions. In 1949, Russell wrote about this in his book on authority and the individual:

> To believe that there can be good and evil in a collection of human beings, over and above the good and evil in the various individuals, is an error; moreover, it is an error which leads straight to totalitarianism, and is therefore dangerous.

(Russell, 1949, p. 89)

Not unlike in 1949, we are living a global reality in which differences in values and perceptions are evident. Differences are a fundamental prerequisite for novelty to emerge. At the same time, differences are also the sources of destructive conflict. The rapid changes, crises, and disasters leaders and employees of organizations experience spurs ever more control in a 'cycle' that rests upon the notion that management, control, routines, and guidelines exist as the tools to be inflicted upon human action.

However, responding to changes in organizations and the managing of critical and unpredictable events are not only dependent on rules and regulations but on bending and breaking them. This creates a paradoxical moral ethical situation for the organization: employees cannot be encouraged to break rules and practices, yet at the same time they must be prepared to do just that in the face of unpredictable and new situations.

Ethics and values are closely related to everyday sensemaking, and can vary greatly within the same organization, regardless of whether a common value ground or ethical guidelines have been decided. The challenge for leaders is to develop a deeper human and organizational understanding for their competent participation in everyday human relating. In order to lead organizations into an open future fraught with uncertainty and change, leaders are challenged to deal with uncontrolled and paradoxical phenomena. Leaders' competence is expressed in how they, together with employees, work under continuous uncertainty.

Leaders' understanding of ethics, ideals, moral, and values are decisive for their organizations (Taylor, 2005). In every group and organization there are norms and attitudes influenced by the people that are most powerful, even if the reality among people can be very different from what the leaders want. In their official documents and statements, the most powerful leaders formulate the wishes and myths to which they want people in their organization to adhere.

Modern ethical theory tends to idealize stability and moral codes, while ignoring the flexibility and change aspects of human beings, and the conflicts of everyday practice (Griffin, 2002, p. 215). The paradox of idealizing and functionalizing morals and ethics is often removed to favour the stable and ideal side of the paradox.

Organizations do not function well if leaders and practitioners lock the paradoxes of morals and ethics into repetitive patterns and only focus on stability. However, in order to be normative (i.e. to decide on one solution instead of another), some contrasts and doubts in situations will need to be removed. At the same time, normative solutions also create new paradoxes, which confront the practitioners.

Potentially, organizations become dysfunctional when the actors do not accept the ongoing paradoxes in organizational interaction dynamics, but instead seek to remove the paradoxes systematically in the same way in many contexts over a long period. This increases the risk of loss of diversity in patterns of action, further giving rise to too much repetition of behaviour, which is characteristic of a neurotic organization (Kets de Vries & Miller, 1984).

Griffin (2002, p. 216) states:

> There is another way of moving from thinking about ethics and leadership entirely in terms of stability, without concluding that they are illusory. One can avoid thinking in terms of ethical universals as "fixed realities" against which human conduct is to be judged, apart from and before action with meaning known in advance. Instead, one can think of ethics as the interpretation of actions to be found in the action itself, in the ongoing recognition of the meanings of actions that could not have been known in advance.

A struggle to keep moral ethical paradoxes alive in organizational practices is a struggle that includes sustaining a tensional movement between known and unknown – between recognizable and unpredictable – the very essence of contexts in which crisis and emergency organizations have to respond.

References

Argyris, C. & Schön, D. (1978). *Organizational Learning: A Theory of Action Perspective*. Reading, MA: Addison-Wesley.

Dalal, F. (1998). *Taking the Group Seriously: Towards a Post-Foulkesian Group Analytic Theory*. London: Jessica Kingsley Press.

Elias, N. (1991). *The Society of Individuals*. Oxford: Blackwell.

Elias, N. & Scotson, J. (1994). *The Established and the Outsiders*. London: Sage.

Griffin, D. (2002). *The Emergence of Leadership: Linking Self-Organization and Ethics*. London: Routledge.

Joas, H. (2000). *The Genesis of Values*. Cambridge: Polity Press.

Kets de Vries, M. F. R. & Miller, D. (1984). *The Neurotic Organization: Diagnosing and Changing Counterproductive Styles of Management*. San Fransisco, CA: Jossey-Bass.

Mead, G. H. (1923). Scientific method and the moral sciences. *International Journal of Ethics*, XVIII, pp. 311–323.

Ouchi, W. G. (1981). *Theory Z: How American Business Can Meet the Japanese Challenge*. Reading, MA: Addison-Wesley.

Russell, B. (1949/1985). *Authority and the Individual*. London: George Allen & Unwin.

Senge, P. M. (1990). *The Fifth Discipline: The Art and Practice of the Learning Organization*. New York: Doubleday.

Stacey, R. D. (2010). *Complexity and Organizational Reality*. London: Routledge.

Taylor, J. (2005). Leadership and cult values: Moving from the idealized to the experienced. In: D. Griffin & R. D. Stacey (eds). *Complexity and the Experience of Leading Organizations*. London: Routledge, pp. 126–150.

Part III
The Military
in International Crisis

8   From the Arctic to Libya

Introduction

In the second case, I present and discuss the response of the Royal Norwegian Air Force (RNoAF) to the Libyan crisis in 2011.[1] The case is a story of the actions of some of the military actors during the first five days of the response. Apart from the top leaders, individuals in the story are kept anonymous. Their military units are abbreviated. Formal English abbreviations are used where they exist; otherwise Norwegian abbreviations are used. A list explaining their meaning is provided in the following section.

Abbreviations and Explanations

AFA   Administrative Service Unit. The unit is responsible for all contracts and administrative procedures concerning deployed troops/capabilities.

LST   The Air Force Staff. The central staff at the RNoAF's Rygge Air Station.

NJHQ   The Norwegian Joint Headquarters are located outside Bodø in Northern Norway. The headquarters are responsible for operational planning, leading, and coordinating all of the Norwegian Armed Forces' operations in peacetime, crisis, and war, both in Norway and abroad.

FST   Defence Staff, based in Oslo.

GIL   In 2011, the Inspector General of the Royal Norwegian Air Force was in charge of development and training of all resources in the RNoAF. The title of the general has since changed to Chief of Air Force.

LOI   Air Force Inspectorate of Operations at Rygge Air Station is responsible for the inspection and approval of operational capability and quality in the RNoAF.

132 LV 132 Air Wing, F-16 fighters stationed at Bodø Air Station, Northern Norway.

NDLO   Norwegian Defence Logistics Organization is responsible for re-
        source planning and coordination of logistics for all branches of
        the Norwegian Armed Forces.

OPG   Operations planning group. A group that is responsible for plan-
        ning a military deployment and operation.

QRA   Quick Reaction Alert. The 132 Air Wing at Bodø Air Station is
        designated for quick response to military activity in Norwegian
        airspace and NATO's northernmost airspace bordering interna-
        tional air space and Russian airspace in the North Atlantic and
        Barents Sea.

Sitsen The Armed Forces Situation Centre at the Ministry of Defence
        in Oslo. The centre is responsible for strategic coordination and
        monitoring of emerging or ongoing military situations or crises. It
        is the central information source in crises for the Chief of Defence
        and Minister of Defence/Government.

Thursday, 17 March 2011

On the evening of Thursday, 17 March 2011, the United Nations Security Council, acting under the authority of Chapter VII of the UN Char-
ter, adopted Resolution 1973 by 10 votes in favour, with none against,
and five abstentions, respectively, from Brazil, Russia, India, China, and
Germany. The resolution demanded immediate ceasefire in Libya and at
the same time approved a no-fly zone over Libya. The Security Council
authorized member states acting either alone or through regional organizations or in coalition to use 'any necessary means' to protect civilians
threatened by attack from military forces within Libya. At the same time,
the Council ruled out any foreign occupant of any kind on Libyan territory. In Norway, the media reported the decision late in the evening of 17
March 2011.

Friday, 18 March 2011

Early in the morning, Norwegian media reported that Norway would participate in a mission against Libya. The Minister of Defence, other politicians, and the Chief of Defence made statements about their interpretations
of how the UN's decision related to Norway's position. They said Norway
would contribute to the operation, but did not clarify what way that would
be done. F-16 fighter jets were mentioned, together with maritime patrol
aircrafts (Orion) and tactical transport planes (C-130 Hercules).

At the same time, phone calls were made between persons who might
contribute to the process within the central command at Rygge Air Station,
the Armed Forces Situation Centre (Sitsen) in Oslo, and 132 Air Wing (132
LV) in Bodø, Northern Norway. 132 LV is on a 15–minute Quick Reaction

Alert (QRA). Their main daily missions are to be ready to identify, observe, and cut off Russian flights along the Norwegian coast and NATO's northern flank. The Russian flights come from bases on the Kola Peninsula in the Russian High North and typically fly along Norway's coast, southwards as far as the coast of the British Isles before returning.

The commanding officer of 132 LV was abroad on vacation when his second–in–command officer was called from the Air Force Staff (LST) at Rygge Air Station and asked to start preparations for the planning and deployment of a F-16 fighter contribution. The commander was asked how much time he would need before an operational force could be ready. He interpreted this question as an indication that the mobilization was a matter of urgency. He could not answer right away, but started to call people whom he thought could contribute. The logistics commander at the air base agreed to support the operation, even though he had not received any orders to do so from his superiors.

In the Norwegian Armed Forces, the Norwegian Defence Logistics Organization (NDLO) is a separate organization with its own chain of command. Formally, therefore, the request for logistics support in the planning of international deployment should have come from the Inspector General of the Royal Norwegian Air Force (GIL)[2] to the Director of NDLO. Orders should then have gone to the commanding NDLO officer at Bodø Air Station before that officer could go ahead with the logistics operation. However, in the event, this whole chain of command was skipped.

Meanwhile, a phone call was made from the Air Force Staff at Rygge to the person they wanted to be Detachment Commander for the international mission. He too was on holiday abroad, but immediately prepared for return to Norway.

At 11:15, the order to start preparations for deployment was given from the Defence Staff (FST) to GIL. No time frame was set.

At the Administrative Service Unit (AFA) at Rygge, the staff reckoned that nothing more would happen during the weekend. The Air Force Inspectorate of Operations (LOI) asked 132 LV to report back by **14:00** how many people and how much cargo they would need in order to cope with one week in the Mediterranean area. 132 LV had already established an operations planning group (OPG). There were no formal decisions by the Government at this time, and little involvement by the Norwegian Joint Headquarters (NJHQ). The nature of the international operation was not clear, and no one knew whether it was a coalition operation, a NATO operation, or which country or organization was to command it.

At NJHQ, staff reckoned that deployment would take place in *10 days* at the earliest. At **12:30**, the planning process started in the OPG at 132 LV. The group consisted of 12 men led by a major, all with experience from similar work. The RNoAF had in 2011 a responsibility for the defence of Iceland's air space and in March 2011 it had conducted exercises for deployment to

Iceland based on an operation plan of 115 persons plus cargo. With the Iceland plan and a map of the Mediterranean on the table, the operations group discussed how fast they could deploy and who should participate.

During the afternoon, many conversations were held across the country, mainly by phone, between people at 132 LV, NJHQ, LOI, and the Defence Staff (FST). At 132 LV, staff started calling people belonging to other relevant organizational units in the Armed Forces. In order to have enough pilots ready to participate, contact was also made with the Air Wing at Ørland Air Base in Central Norway. The leader of the OPG discussed the weapons cargo issue with his contact person in LOI, without involving the NJHQ at that time.

During the evening, the leader of the OPG joined some colleagues from a visiting squadron for a beer in the bar. He asked whether he could borrow the Hercules C-130 transport plane they had parked on the base, since that would make things much easier for the deployment. The use of resources such as the C-130 was controlled by the NJHQ, but the men in the bar agreed to hand over the plane to 132 LV. Meanwhile at the NJHQ, an order to proceed with planning had been received; the order stated 'deployment in 10 days'.

At **23:45**, an early warning order for 132 LV to prepare for deployment ticked in from the chief of LOI. 132 LV had already spent 18 hours preparing for deployment.

Saturday, 19 March 2011

In Bodø, work continued and a large network of people was in operation. The appointed Detachment Commander had arrived in Bodø and participated in the planning process of the OPG. About 200 people were working on the logistics process. The local leaders made contact with all 120 personnel who were to be deployed. For international operations, personnel must volunteer. Usually, a 28-day warning is required for international operations, but the Chief of Defence had made an exception in this case. The personnel did not file the status of their teeth for possible later identification and they did not test their personal weapons, despite both procedures were required in international operations.

However, GIL told the OPG staff not to let administrative requirements and budgets hold them back. This was interpreted by them as yet one more signal that they were about to embark on an urgent deployment and that approval by GIL meant approval by the Chief of Defence, Minister of Defence, and the Government for the operation to proceed regardless of bureaucratic routines.

At Sitsen, there was frequent phone contact with 132 LV. Both the Chief of Defence and the Minister of Defence regularly stopped off at Sitsen, given that their offices were in close proximity; but rather than interfering with the operational work, their prime concern was the command of the forces in the operation. They did not signal a time frame or degree of urgency. There were three Lieutenant Colonels in Sitsen, among them the contact person from LOI. At one point, he received a call from a colleague in Belgium, who told him that the Belgians were sending a site survey team from Brussels to Araxos, Greece, on Sunday afternoon, and that the Norwegians could join if they wanted. This meant they would have to send a team from Bodø on Sunday morning (i.e. within the next 24 hours). The team was quickly put together by the OPG at 132 LV, regardless of the NJHQ.

Meanwhile, about 15–20 logistics people had arrived at work at the NJHQ, but it was hard for them to gain an overview of what was happening. They were under the impression that they were in a NATO mission, although this had not been confirmed.

In Paris, a lunchtime meeting in the Élysée Palace was being held between European state leaders, including the Norwegian Prime Minister, to discuss their position in relation to the 1973 UN resolution. Some countries, most importantly France and the UK, accepted the implementation of the UN resolution. Norway announced its support and participation. It was at this time that it became clear politically that there would be a military operation against Libya and that Norway would actually participate in it. However, no one knew what type of operation it was going to be or who would command it.

At 13:30, a videoconference was held, this time between GIL, a senior officer from LOI, the leader of the 132 LV's OPG, the 132 LV's second-in-command, and the chief logistics officer of 132 LV. The atmosphere in the meeting was informal and relaxed, and the participants used each other's first names when they talked to each other. Titles and 'Sir' are not usually used in verbal communication in Norwegian culture, not even in the military. GIL informed that it was official that the Chief of Defence wanted to send F-16s. No one from the NJHQ attended the meeting, but it was noted that the NJHQ still wanted to use the Orion.

GIL informed that the formal order would come soon. The participants in the meeting agreed to bring the 'whole package', which meant a combination of all available weapons. GIL asked for an estimate of the time when they could leave, and when he was told about the Belgians who were leaving from Brussels at 15:00 on Sunday, he agreed to deploy first and make ready for operations afterwards, which was the opposite of normal procedure.

During the afternoon, the Commander of 132 LV had arrived back from his holiday, but he let the group led by the major carry on their work without interfering or taking command. He remained present and briefed about the situation during the day.

At 18:13, the formal order to deploy came by e-mail to all relevant units. However, there was still no time frame for the operation. The local logistics commander, a lieutenant colonel who had been deeply involved in the preparation work thus far, wanted to join the first team to Greece on Sunday morning and thought it best to call his superior in Oslo and tell him about it. His superior responded that he had no information to indicate urgency. However, the lieutenant colonel said he was going anyway. Several weeks later, he received a formal order to deploy with the first team.

Sunday, 20 March 2011

At 09:00, a 'borrowed' Hercules took off from Bodø Air Station with the site survey team on-board. They landed in Oslo to pick up the leader of the team, and then the team travelled onwards to Brussels, met up with the Belgians, and then flew to Araxos.

Later in the day, 132 LV in Bodø received a deployment order from the NJHQ. The order was based on a NATO operation. They sent the order back and asked the NJHQ to write another order because they were not participating in a NATO operation. In fact, no one knew what type of operation it was, which made it difficult for any orders to be written.

Meanwhile, three senior officers were presenting a series of 30-minute information briefings to different groups who were to be deployed from the air station. The officers talked about the operation, technical matters, and conditions of deployment, and took time to answer any questions. The leader of the OPG was in a videoconference for further clarification of the terms for the crew. At that point, the commander of the NJHQ arrived at the headquarters and was briefed on activities thus far. The staff at the NJHQ now realized that the F-16 fighter planes would be deployed the following day.

At 14:00, a press conference was held in Bodø, at which the commanding officer of 132 LV, the Detachment Commander, and the leader of the OPG informed the public about the ongoing deployment. The NJHQ did not attend.

Around midnight, the site survey team arrived at Araxos and immediately arranged for a meeting with the Belgians and the Greeks. During the meeting, it became clear that there were restrictions on flying from Araxos Air Base: they could not do night flights. The Norwegian team was planning for 24-hour flying operations, and now had to consider whether it would be better to go to the airbase at Souda Bay, Crete.

A slight tension erupted during the meeting between the Belgian commander and the Norwegians. There seemed to be some military cultural differences. The Norwegian officers did not like the Belgian commander's attitude towards the Greeks; they saw him as authoritarian and demanding. The Norwegians wanted to invite collaboration, since they were guests on Greek soil. Major military geopolitics had suddenly arrived on Crete and there had to be some recognition of the sensitivity of the mission, for which they knew they would need all the help with practical matters they could get from the local Cretan community. The Araxos base lacked much of the necessary infrastructure for military operations, such as housing and food supplies. The Souda base would probably also become crowded, so the officers would be dependent on local civilian facilities and help. There were also security issues, both for the locals and for the soldiers, issues that could not be easily handled without cooperation. The site survey team needed to secure the trust and support of the local community. The Norwegian officers left the meeting with the Belgian commander. They would sleep on the decision whether to stay at Araxos.

Monday, 21 March 2011

In the morning, the operational forces at 132 LV were reported clear for deployment. Command was formally transferred from GIL to the NJHQ. At 09:00, the F-16s took off from Bodø without any clear destination. Although the planes were already on their way and under NJHQ's command, the officers at the NJHQ continued to discuss which base to use. After conversations with the site survey team at Araxos, NJHQ decided that the operation should be based at Souda Bay, Crete.

The information that the F-16s were being directed to the Souda Bay airbase was supposed to have been given to the F-16 pilots via the crew of their tanker aircraft somewhere over Europe, but the tanker crew misunderstood and instead directed the F-16s to Sicily. On their approach to Sigionella Naval Air Station in Sicily, the F-16s were denied permission to land because the airbase could not handle any more planes. Instead, the RNoAF's planes ended up in Sardinia, where they received an order from the NJHQ *not* to land in Sicily.

Meanwhile, the site survey team arrived at the Souda Bay airbase and a meeting was immediately set up between them, the Belgians, and the Greeks. This time, the meeting was more successful. The Greeks helped the Norwegians to take care of a number of crucial practical matters that had to be in place for the operational force to settle on the base as quickly as possible. Notice was given to the F-16s that the Souda Bay airbase was 'OK'. During the day, the administration at Bodø Air Station had produced and prepared the documents necessary to clarify and deploy the personnel, including for those who had already departed.

In the evening, the RNoAF's F-16s arrived at Souda Bay, Crete, and the crew continued preparations for their first mission over Libya, which happened just three days later. Since the start of preparations and until their arrival on Crete – a process that according to procedure should take weeks – it had taken three days, and only two days after the formal political decision was made in Paris, for the RNoAF to respond to the rapidly emerging international crisis in Libya.

Notes

1 The case material was obtained together with Dr. Bjørner B. Christensen as part of a research project financed by the RNoAF between 2011 and 2012. The present case is based on declassified material.
2 GIL is the general in charge of the RNoAF until any elements of the force are formally handed over for operational command to the Norwegian Joint Headquarters (NJHQ), located outside Bodø. The function of the general has since been changed to Chief of Air Force.

9   Strategy Theory

This chapter is an intermezzo between the case description and the further analysis of it. The purpose is to provide a short background to the most relevant parts of strategy theory, and discuss some of the problems traditional theories face in relation to widespread experiences of complexity and unpredictable breakdowns in organized patterns of behaviour. I will attempt to address these problems by arguing for a complexity theoretical approach to strategy theory in which strategies are understood as coherent patterns of action emerging in organizational practices. Because these practices differ, there can be no common understanding of strategies and strategic leadership or management. These terms are constructed and found in the experience of people in practices. Strategy as bureaucratic practice, therefore, is different from strategy as operational practice.

Origins of Military Strategy

The concept of strategy has its origins in the military. Historically we might think of army generals and conquerors like Alexander the Great and Julius Cesar as founders of strategy as practical ways of using armies to win battles and wars. Strategy is in this sense closely linked to planning activities of generals who want to (1) build the military capabilities that will enable them to win wars and control territories; and (2) use the military capabilities in ways that will outsmart the enemy's strategy in case of war.

As theory, strategy literature refers as far back as the Chinese general Sun-tzu's book *The Art of War*, written sometime between 400 and 300 BC (Sun-tzu, 2011). In the modern age, the book *Vom Kriege (On War)*, originally written by the Prussian General von Clausewitz in 1832, is still much referred as the classical work on military strategy (von Clausewitz, 1989).

Of the ten different schools of thought in strategy theory categorized by Mintzberg, Ahlstrand & Lampel (1998), *the positioning school* has its origins in the military and is seen in the work of both Sun-tzu and von

Clausewitz. What the school promotes is, in the words of Mintzberg, Ahlstrand & Lampel (1998, pp. 89–90):

> ... notably the need for clear deliberate strategy, the centrality of authority to develop or at least execute that strategy, the need to keep strategy simple, and the presumed proactive nature of strategic management.

The key aspect of the positioning school is not only to emphasize the need for strategies to be in the form of plans and designs, but that there are only a few strategies or positions that can be used as defence against an enemy or a competitor. Strategies must fit the particular position that the organization wants to take in order to win over the opponents.

Strategy and Decision-making

From the 1950s onwards, the concept of strategy became popular with political and business leaders as a form of long-term decision-making in public and private organizations. The idea was that organizational and societal futures could be chosen, planned, and designed on the basis of rational analyses of the past and the present. This created the grounds for the concept of strategic planning (Ansoff, 1965), which promotes strategy as a very formalized process where everything in the organization should be planned and fitted into each other, almost as in a machine. Strategies should be formed from a controlled, conscious process, overseen by the top leader, and appear as detailed plans to be implemented through objectives, budgets, programmes, and operating plans (Mintzberg, 1994).

However, already in 1945, Herbert Simon had demonstrated the limitations of rational decision-making (Simon, 1945). It became quite clear that decision-making in organizations could not be completely rational and well-informed choices between all possible alternatives. Rather, as elaborated by March & Simon (1958), decisions are bounded rational because humans have limited capacity to process information, limited access to information, and limited influence on each other's views in political processes.

Rational and Bounded Rational Choice

Allison (1971) studied the political strategic decision-making processes during the Cuban Missile Crisis in 1962 and found that standard procedures played an important role in the behaviour of the decision-makers. Even if the situation was new to the actors, their earlier habits when approaching problems and crises guided them in their decision-making.

Anderson (1983) concluded that goals and choices between alternatives in the Cuban Missile Crisis emerged from the social interaction between the actors. The participants did not review many options at the same time, but rather discussed one option at a time. In the crisis, many sought alternatives that they thought would reduce the risk, rather than alternatives that could solve the situation. Hickson et al. (1986) have shown that decision-making processes become more diffuse as the complexity and the political context of the decisions increase. Threatening environments, a high degree of uncertainty, and external control all lead to less rationality in the decisions.

Janis (1982) described the pattern of 'groupthink', a phenomenon wherein consensus is sought and recreated within a group. Janis considered groupthink an expression of reduced rationality. In order to avoid this, he recommended the introduction of a devil's advocate in the group to increase the level of conflict. This can be done either by inviting external experts into the discussions or by leaders encouraging more in-depth discussions. However, if the level of conflict increases in a group, it risks interfering with otherwise collaborative working relations. The acceptance and motivation for individuals to follow up and implement decisions could be negatively affected.

In groups with strong internal dependencies between group members, such as the police and military, it is conceivable that they will accept low levels of creativity in operational contexts as a trade-off against the risk of dividing the group. Groups in which leaders have a strong inclination towards stability, discipline, control, and authority will risk sacrificing the best decisions for the sake of keeping the harmony of the group. Such group dynamics can create problems during emergencies and crises.

A number of studies have revealed negative correlations between rationality in the decision-making process and performance in unstable contexts, and positive correlation in stable environments (Fredrickson, 1984; Fredrickson & Mitchell, 1984; Fredrickson & Iaquinto, 1989). Coherent, planned, and controlled decision processes seem to be of little relevance when environments undermine the planning. In such circumstances, it is better, not least for leaders, to spend their time adapting to the emerging situations.

Fast and Slow Decision-making: Constructed Rationality and Intuition

Rational decision-making is associated with slow decision-making because it encourages the collection of large amounts of information, analyses, and consideration of alternatives based on the information. By contrast, intuitive decision-making is associated with speed, limited information, 'gut feeling', and local immediate response (Kahnemann, 2013).

Although organizational practices vary, the phenomena of intuition and rationality are not easily separated. Unlike practices, intuition and rationality are universal human phenomena. Hence, there is no a priori reason to believe that decision-makers in different practices differ in their individual capacity for rational and intuitive behaviour when they participate in the practices and processes of organizations.

However, the need for speed differs with different practices. Leader's experiences will make them behave differently, although it is not clear whether this necessarily leads to better or worse decisions. In studies of management behaviour, Kotter (1982) rarely observed managers making decisions. According to Kotter decisions emerged from a fluid and confusing series of conversations, meetings, and memorandums based on intuition and experience.

These findings concur with the description originally given by Lindblom (1959) of decision-making as 'muddling through'. Mintzberg, Ahlstrand & Lampel (1998) calls this way of thinking about strategy the 'learning school', suggesting that leaders learn from whatever is happening and then adapt their plans quickly in discussions about their organization's future.

In strategy research, this idea became coherent from the 1970s onwards by a number of studies from Mintzberg and colleagues. They suggested that strategies as organizational reality are not the result of rational plans and choices by leaders, but rather evolve over time as a result of interactions between planning activities and responses to unpredictable events. Hence, organizational activities are the results of combinations of plans and emergent events. Real strategies are fusions of deliberate and emergent strategies (Mintzberg & Waters, 1985).

Eisenhardt (1989) found that effective decision-makers tended to come up with many alternatives when faced with a problematic situation, while they actually followed few of the alternatives. She interpreted these findings as evidence of both rational and intuitive behaviour at the same time. It seems leaders do not act purely rationally, bounded rationally, or intuitively, but rather adapt their rationality in complex ways to the situation in which they find themselves.

Political Processes and Ideological Adaptation

The political perspective on strategic decision-making is founded on the understanding that decisions are the result of negotiations and conflicts between actors with different goals and interests. Outcomes are dependent on coalitions and power games between people with different interests, practices, and ambitions. Strategic decisions tend to follow the interests of those who are most powerful (March, 1962; Salancik & Pfeffer, 1974). People involve themselves in political tactics in order to increase their influence. This does not mean that most people prefer to engage in conflicts and power struggles. If the aim is to increase influence over decisions, political behaviour could equally be directed towards collaboration as confrontation.

Organized Anarchy and Randomness

The 'garbage can' model was first developed by Cohen, March & Olsen (1972) and refers to decisions made in conflicting environments and what the authors termed organized anarchies. The model is a reaction to the smooth rational models, and is an attempt to describe political games further when the environments are complex, unstable, and diffuse.

The garbage can alternative emphasizes chance, luck, and timing as important factors in how things play out. Eisenhardt & Zbaracki (1992) noted that the garbage can model does not have sufficient empirical evidence to support it. Ideological criteria remained stable over time, which indicates that the observed changes were not as random as they seemed, and rather that changes happen as adaptations to sustain an underlying ideological view.

Eisenhardt & Zbaracki (1992) summarized that empirical studies conducted prior to the early 1990s had suggested that strategic decision-making is best described as a combination of bounded rational behaviour and political behaviour. Bounded rationality limits the kind of information decision-makers can absorb, and political behaviour forms the social context in which decisions are made. Although the garbage can model can be used to describe certain cases, it does not have much empirical support. The seemingly messy and random organizational development that it traces over time cannot be explained by claiming that people's actions are more or less random. The theory lacks an explanation of how, over time, individual actors who are operating rationally and intuitively in organized contexts produce what seems to be randomness.

Rethinking Strategy

Since the 1990s, events have dramatically increased the need to rethink strategy, operational management, and leadership. Developments such as the fall of communist regimes in the Soviet Union and Eastern Europe around 1990; the rise and influence of the Internet, global communication technologies, and media; the global financial collapse in 2008 and the subsequent economic downturn in many parts of the world; and the Arab Spring of 2011 cannot be explained using the traditional wisdom of strategic planning. The patterns are rather expressions of the complex, radical, and unpredictable dynamics of the world, a dynamism that demands new explanations and theories as well as new views on strategies, operational capabilities, and leadership practices in emergency organizations, practices that are responding to a world ingrained with crises and unforeseen events.

Recently, strategy researchers have recognized that there is a lack of knowledge of the relationships between strategy, politics, culture, and practice (Clegg et al., 2011) and that research needs to be directed towards how strategies come about as practice (Jarzabkowski, 2003; Whittington, 2006; Johnson et al., 2007; MacIntosh & MacLean, 2014).

Stacey (2011) has developed a theory of organization in which he calls for strategy theory to be founded in a combination of complexity theory's descriptions of evolving self-organizing patterns, and social theory based on the ideas of Mead (1934) and Elias (1939). In Stacey's complex responsive processes theory, strategy is seen as the emergence of identity in organizations. Organizational identity emerges in communicative interactions between a large number of people who are included and excluded in social group patterns. Leaders who are thinking about strategy are but a few of these people who are immersed in these patterns, which means that although leaders do influence strategies as patterns of action, they cannot control them. Even in cases where leaders have dictatorial political power to force large-scale changes upon a society, attempts to control what is going to happen in many (perhaps most) cases have been counterproductive, and in some cases catastrophic (Scott, 1998).

When it comes to contexts of crisis and emergency, the pioneering research of Karl Weick (Weick, 1988; 2001) describes culturally constructed understanding and sensemaking in operational organizations under conditions of stress and crisis. However, the suggestion to create *high-reliability organizations* (Weick & Sutcliffe, 2007) in order to 'manage the unexpected' tends to echo what Mintzberg, Ahlstrand & Lampel (1998) called *the design school* within strategic management. This school of strategy goes back to Selznick (1957) and Chandler (1962), who argued for a need to harmonize the organization's internal state with the external expectations, or threats, from the environment. Strategy in this way of thinking has to do with prescriptions for a kind of designed organizational stability that is illusionary.

Therefore, despite efforts since the 1970s to understand organizational strategies as emergent cultural processes rather than as rational decision-making, planning, and design, there seems to be a 'missing link' between operational leadership and the literature on strategic management and organizational dynamics. Much is still undone in strategy theory when it comes to combining new and different aspects of organizational and leadership knowledge with the realities of organizational practice. Groups' and individuals' rationality, creativity, and intuition are not identical in all contexts, even though they are universal human phenomena. These phenomena, which are thought to drive decision-making processes, emerge and are interpreted within group and organizational practices and within complex social interactions, none of which are predictable but are nevertheless decisive for the functionality and development of organizations.

Thus, theories of strategic and operational leadership lack explanations of how organized contexts that are constructed with hierarchies, formal responsibilities, and clear-cut operational levels can still evolve completely unpredictably. How can this unpredictability emerge from ordinary and organized practice, in which actions are routinely repeated?

Complexity Theory

Two phenomena described by complexity theorists are particularly important and relevant to organizational strategy theory: self-organization and emergent processes. When seen as social interaction, both phenomena result from interactions that emerge as a consequence of communication between people. Self-organization is an interactional process whereby individual and collective identity emerges and changes. Plans, rules, routines, and procedures are not the causes or prescriptions for future action, but are part of the way people interact and communicate and therefore they are part of power and organizational patterns. In this regard, the plans and tools used by leaders are technologies that, together with leader's intentions, are involved in the communication and negotiations of influence and support in organizations.

In these processes, it is possible for unplanned events and situations to emerge as a result of what has been going on between different actors. Although activities and events might seem random and surprising from the perspective of the individual, they nevertheless happen because of people's actions. Individual human actions are not always easy to understand, to gain an overview of, or to know the full background to, because they are both restrained and enabled by conscious and unconscious relational power phenomena. Organizations, which are large patterns of human *inter*actions, are even more complex to understand, let alone control.

To move the discussion of strategy from powerful individuals' choices and intentions, or seeing them as more or less random coincidences, towards viewing strategies as emerging individual and collective identities resulting from ongoing interactions and power relations between people represents a shift. Both conscious and unconscious choices, as well as ethical and unethical actions, emerge paradoxically at the same time in relations between people. Strategies are not always 'slow' decision-making and planning leading to even slower implementation. During crises and emergencies, strategies can emerge very rapidly in response to whatever is happening. Sometimes, hierarchically speaking, strategies are translated into practice before they are decided, and they may be translated into plans after they have emerged as practice. Thus, they can be time-reversed plans about the past rather than the future.

The Meaning of Strategic Management in Different Practices

If strategies and strategic knowledge are created in everyday actions (i.e. as practices), it will be problematic to differentiate between the formulation and implementation of strategies as phases in a strategy process. The division between formulation and implementation is a division of practices. Divisions of practices create problems when a strategy formulated by senior management is to be carried out by middle management. These two groups of managers perform different practices; their work is simply different. Therefore, as practices, strategies must be different too. Consequently, strategies decided at a 'higher level' in a hierarchy cannot exist or be carried out at a 'lower level' because the different levels are different practices that hold different realities for the practitioners. The strategies are thus formulated and understood differently in different organizational practices.

Organizational practices are not only driven by rationality but are also activities in which social and individual mechanisms are mobilized in order to preserve identity. At the same time, identity is flexible in the sense that most people tolerate a certain amount of variation in their functional practice (Mead, 1934). Moreover, some practices are more flexible than others, not least during crises and emergencies.

For senior managers, a strategy typically takes the form of a visionary plan for the future. Such managers act politically in a power game wherein coercion, persuasion, and negotiation are carried out to gain support for visionary ideas among board members, middle management, and employees. Some succeed in creating positive engagement for their visions, while many do not. By contrast, middle managers engage in a practice directed towards operational activity. They derive meaning from a strategic plan as long as it is aligned with sensible operational actions.

Strategic management as practice can, in general, be seen as a process of participation in conversations on important emerging themes. In a bureaucratic practice, this activity is aimed at creating coordinated ideal images of a future free of conflict. In an operational practice, the activity is aimed at creating coordinated experiences of a concrete and conflicting present.

Thus, that which is referred to as strategic management expresses the different cultural activities in a bureaucratic practice in tension with an operational practice. There are big differences between these practices. A bureaucratic practice is dominated by abstract written communication, whereas an operational practice is dominated by concrete oral communication. A bureaucratic practice is a rule-based, generalized, and idealized practice, whereas an operational practice is a practice occupied with detailed everyday conflict in need of practical solutions.

Strategic management as bureaucratic practice is a practice detached from operational activity, whereas strategic management as operational practice is an involved, problem-solving practice. Whereas bureaucratic strategies are ideal, static, and seek objectivity, equality, and consistency, operational strategies are unreliable, messy, but yet functional and pragmatic. Consequently, there is no objective meaning to strategic management. The meaning of the idea varies, depending on the practice.

If, independently of practices, strategies were to be carried out without variation, then *either* the operational practice would become a bureaucratic practice, which would leave the operational practice inefficient and dysfunctional, *or* the bureaucratic practice would be reduced to benefitting a purely operational regime, which would disable the function of the bureaucracy as executor of laws, rules, and procedures. Hence, in any sound organizational sense, it is inevitable that the two different practices emerge as conflicting patterns of action.

Non-Linearity and Breakdown of Hierarchy

In organizational contexts, crises and breakdowns in organizations can occur despite the existence of hierarchies and formal structures. Hierarchies are ways of organizing work and responsibility along a top-down dimension, assuming that what is happening in the organization develops in accordance with a direct (linear) cause and effect. When hierarchies break down in a crisis, it is because organizational realities do not evolve in linear, but in complex ways. Connections between cause and effects are non-linear.

Implications of Non-linearity for Strategy

Non-linearity means that small local changes can escalate into large and widespread changes that simultaneously move in different directions. The uprising in North African countries in 2011 was ignited in Tunisia, but spread very rapidly to a number of other countries.

However, the spread developed entirely differently in these countries. For example, in Tunisia there was a relatively peaceful transition to a democratization process, while in Syria there was a total breakdown into years of civil war. Non-linearity also means that grand initiatives can result in little change. NATO has fought the Taliban movement in Afghanistan for more than a decade as a response to terrorism in the West. In 2017, the terror threat still persists, and the Taliban have not disappeared from Afghanistan.

Complex dynamics and non-linearity mean that the escalations of small initiatives are connected to the concentration of large initiatives. Large resources directed towards one area will open up opportunities that can be exploited by smaller groups. The variation in patterns of communication between relatively few and less powerful people can be amplified and spread in ways that undermine the powerful actors' control and horizon of understanding. One example of this is the phenomenon of the terror network 'Islamic State' (IS).

In the aftermath of the uprising in Syria and the withdrawal of a large portion of US military forces from Iraq, grounds were left open for IS activities. A few years earlier, IS had been a marginal group without support and resources, but within a relatively short period of time it became an organization with massive support and access to resources that once again dragged the West into war in the region.

Western security strategies were adapted to what was perceived to be a changed pattern of threat. These changed strategies represented changed patterns of behaviour. They defined what people inside and outside security organizations would be expected to do. Western military strategies were effectively decided by the IS. Hence, in these organizations, the leaders do not control the strategies, because the strategies are dynamic and relational responses to what others, such as military enemies, are doing.

Thus, strategies are responses to other actors' strategies, which in turn are responses to yet other actors' strategies, and so on, in an endless interactional process. Such strategic responses are interpreted and understood in different ways in societies and large organizations, and the strategies therefore become localized and operationally different within the same organization.

Even if the strategies are fragmented on a small scale, given sufficient time, the patterns of action will seem relatively coordinated on a large scale.

References

Allison, G. T. (1971). *Essence of Decision: Explaining the Cuban Missile Crisis*. Boston, MA: Little Brown.

Anderson, P. A. (1983). Decision making by objection and the Cuban Missile Crisis. *Administrative Science Quarterly*, 28, pp. 201–222.

Ansoff, H. I. (1965). *Corporate Strategy*. New York: McGraw-Hill.

Chandler, A. D. Jr (1962). *Strategy and Structure: Chapters in the History of the Industrial Enterprise*. Cambridge, MA: MIT Press.

Clegg, S., Carter, C., Kornberger, M. & Schweitzer, J. (2011). *Strategy: Theory and Practice*. London: Sage.

Cohen, M. S., March, J. G. & Olsen, J. P. (1972). A garbage can model of organizational choice. *Administrative Science Quarterly*, 17, pp. 1–25.

Eisenhardt, K. M. (1989). Making fast strategic decisions in high-velocity environments. *Academy of Management Journal*, 32, pp. 543–576.

Eisenhardt, K. M. & Zbaracki, M. J. (1992). Strategic decision making. *Strategic Management Journal*, 13, pp. 17–37.

Elias, N. (1939/2000). *The Civilizing Process*. Oxford: Blackwell.

Fredrickson, J. W. (1984). The comprehensiveness of strategic decision processes: Extention, observations, future directions. *Academy of Management Journal*, 27, pp. 445–466.

Fredrickson, J. W. & Iaquinto, A. L. (1989). Inertia and creeping rationality in strategic decision processes. *Academy of Management Journal*, 32, pp. 516–542.

Fredrickson, J. W. & Mitchell, T. R. (1984). Strategic decision processes: Comprehensiveness and performance in an industry with an unstable environment. *Administrative Science Quarterly*, 27, pp. 399–423.

Hickson, D. J., Butler, R. J., Cray, D., Mallory, G. R. & Wilson, D. C. (1986). *Top Decisions: Strategic Decision-Making in Organizations*. San Francisco, CA: Jossey-Bass.

Janis, I. L. (1982). *Groupthink: Psychological Studies of Policy Decisions and Fiascoes*. 2nd ed. Boston, MA: Wadsworth, Cengage Learning.

Jarzabkowski, P. (2003). Strategic practices: An activity theory perspective on continuity and change. *Journal of Management Studies*, 40, pp. 23–55.

Johnson, G., Langley, A., Melin, L. & Whittington, R. (2007). *Strategy as Practice: Research Directions and Resources*. Cambridge: Cambridge University Press.

Kahneman, D. (2013). *Thinking, Fast and Slow*. New York: Farrar, Straus & Giroux.

Kotter, J. P. (1982). *The General Managers*. New York: Free press.

Lindblom, C. E. (1959). The science of muddling through. *Public Administration Review*, 19, pp. 79–88.

MacIntosh, R. & MacLean, D. (2014). *Strategic Management: Strategists at Work*. London: Palgrave Macmillan.

March, J. G. (1962). The business firm as a political coalition. *The Journal of Politics*, 24, pp. 662–678.

March, J. G. & Simon, H. A. (1958/1993). *Organizations*. 2nd ed. Cambridge, MA: Blackwell.

Mead, G. H. (1934). *Mind, Self and Society*. Chicago: Chicago University Press.

Mintzberg, H. (1994). *The Rise and Fall of Strategic Planning: Reconceiving Roles for Planning, Plans, Planner*. New York: The Free Press.

Mintzberg, H., Ahlstrand, B. & Lampel, J. (1998). *Strategy Safari*. New York: The Free Press.

Mintzberg, H. & Waters, J. A. (1985). Of strategies, deliberate and emergent. *Strategic Management Journal*, 6, pp. 257–272.

Salancik, G. R. & Pfeffer, J. (1974). The bases and use of power in organizational decision making: The case of a university budget. *Administrative Science Quarterly*, 19, pp. 453–473.

Scott, J. C. (1998). *Seeing Like a State: How Certain Schemes to Improve the Human Condition Have Failed*. New Haven, CT: Yale University Press.

Selznick, P. (1957). *Leadership in Administration: A Sociological Interpretation*. Evanston, IL: Row, Peterson.

Simon, H. (1945). *Administrative Behavior: A Study of Decision-Making Processes in Administrative Organization*. New York: Palgrave Macmillan.

Stacey, R. D. (2011). *Strategic Management & Organisational Dynamics: The Challenge of Complexity*. 6th ed. London: Pearson Education Ltd.

Sun-tzu (2011). *The Art of War*. London: Amber Books Ltd.

von Clausewitz, C. (1989). *On War*, M. E. Howard & P. Paret (ed. and trans.). Princeton, NJ: Princeton University Press.

Weick, K. E. (1988). Enacted sense making in crisis situations. *Journal of Management Studie*s, 25(4), pp. 305–317.

Weick, K. E. (2001). *Making Sense of Organization*. Malden, MA: Blackwell.

Weick, K. E. & Sutcliffe, K. (2007). *Managing the Unexpected: Resilient Performance in an Age of Uncertainty*. San Francisco, CA: Jossey-Bass.

Whittington, R. (2006). Completing the practice turn in strategy research. *Organization Studies*, 27(5), pp. 613–634.

10 Network Strategies and Complexity

In this chapter, I will move on to discuss how, in the wake of the recent decade's global military experiences, military organizations have adopted ideas of networks and complexity in their strategic thinking. I discuss how these ideas are not straightforward, because, although dressed up as new ideas, some of the concepts are framed and kept within well-known boundaries of traditional strategic thinking. With a particular view to the Libya case, this leads to a discussion of what complexity thinking means for strategy, organization, and leadership in military organizations.

A New Global Reality

It is clear that the shifting global realities faced by Western military organizations challenge traditional ideas of organization, leadership, and strategy. As recent experience of the emergence of the armed conflicts in Libya, Syria, the rise of the Islamic State in Iraq and Syria, and the Russian intervention in Ukraine has brutally demonstrated, the missions and conflicts that Western military organizations must be ready to deal with feature fuzzy landscapes between crisis, emergency, terror, and local armed conflicts, which have the potential to rapid escalate and spread.

So far, 21st century experiences have demonstrated the blurred boundaries between terrorism and war, and formed a picture of a radically new world situation that demands new ways of thinking about strategy and organizing. Discussions include concepts such as hybrid warfare (Hoffman, 2007) and the necessity for Western military to understand the consequences of complexity, non-linearity, and network organizing. As observed by Fleming (2011, p. 60):

> the U.S. military has collectively struggled to characterize and conceptualize the contemporary flood of non-linear threat activities that resemble more of a spider web rather than a hierarchal layer cake. The resultant strategic confusion and semantic discourse have muddied the waters of threat analysis and conceptual planning.

The core of the arguments is that the military organizations need to become flexible and dynamic in their response to rapid change and emergent unpredictability in the world. Attention must shift from static and fully informed analysis to dynamic and creative analysis, from ordered global military dominance to flexible local response. Metaphorically, military organizations need to be seen as networks of relations rather than monolithic hierarchies.

The congruent shift of strategic thinking has both in the Norwegian and other Western contexts promoted that military organizations must move from (1) static, collective invasion defences to dynamic, specialized reaction defences; (2) hierarchical structures to non-hierarchical networks; and (3) leadership informed by clearly formulated strategies to dynamic, flexible, and reflexive leadership that is responding to immediate emerging objectives and intentions.

Network Strategies, Technology, and Complexity

Network-centric warfare (NCW) is a much debated and central concept that relates to the interactions between technology and personnel in modern warfare (Gomez, 2010). Arntzen & Grøtan (2011) offer a critical discussion of the concept of NCW, in which they argue that the practice emerged before the theory in this field. They warn against an overrated belief in technology and that network thinking carries all signs of being a management fad, based on:

> the fantasy that information and communication technology makes a fundamental difference [but must] pay attention to the premises of human interaction and sensemaking in a context of complexity.
>
> (Arntzen & Grøtan, 2011, p. 257)

Various complexity-inspired theories may seem prone to accepting the idea of organizations as networks. However, complexity theoretical understanding of networks also varies. In general, organizational complexity theories view organizations as ongoing interaction processes between people, wherein networks of entangled technologies are involved in the interaction processes and the patterning of people's actions in a range of different ways.

Cilliers (2001) discussed the usefulness of network models in understanding complex entities and suggested that these models are subject to the same limitations as all models of complexity. Such limitations are due to the need for pre-design and control of the network. If a network should not be left to its own dynamics, some initial parameters have to influence its way of functioning. By introducing such parameters, the network will potentially be limited to pre-set functions, such as those of a formal hierarchy and role system, but simultaneously the limitations will potentially hinder the type of flexibility the network needs in order to take advantage of that way of organizing.

Even if technological networks are identical in technological terms regardless of people, when they are transformed into patterns of human action (i.e. practice), they will be understood in multiple ways, depending on persons and groups. When technologies are introduced into human practice, they become subject to human variation. If we adopt Mead's term 'social objects' for describing human patterning processes, then technologies are also social objects (i.e. patterns of behaviour) (Johannessen & Stacey, 2005).

At the outset, technologies might seem neutral, but they take on variation from the moment humans introduce them in their practices. Similarly, we should assume that not only technologies, but also the information they mediate to different people would be understood differently because information is a social object too. In other words, different persons tend to perceive the same information differently.

Additionally, differences in the social objects of network technologies are produced by variations in levels of investments across the network and different actors having different competencies in dealing with crucial network technologies. Differences also occur in local and national networks, and internationally between allied nations' networks.

Spontaneous coalitions that emerge in response to rapidly evolving conflicts, such as in the Libyan crisis in 2011, can further amplify differences. In the case of the RNoAF's response to the crisis, decisions to join a coalition were made without exactly knowing the level of co-training between the involved partners. Even between close allies, the use of technological resources differs, and more so between shifting coalitions. During the Libya operation they had to settle with a common denominator of communication technology that was 'WW2 standard', as some pilots put it. We also saw this drift towards 'low-tech' human contact in the preparatory phase when within the RNoAF they were communicating mostly through phones and face-to-face talk.

Nevertheless, there is reason to pay attention to the fact that more advanced technology increases non-linearity and complexity in the networks and consequently in the organizational networks under discussion here. It is not the case that technology stays static and manageable, while humans are dynamic and unmanageable. Especially when we talk about interactive technologies, the same interactional phenomena appear as when people interact. We find self-organization, emergence, non-linearity, and paradoxes also in interactive technological networks (Dekker, Cilliers & Hofmeyr, 2011).

In the case of the Libyan operation, information was shared, but the same information did not flow to all involved actors. There was no common situational awareness and understanding based on widely shared information. Rather, there were large differences in the perceptions of the situation, for example between the NJHQ and 132 LV. Many personnel experienced good collaboration, not necessarily because of a common understanding of the situation but rather because they knew and trusted each other. Thus, efficiency in the operation became a fluid measure because some thought the operation went too fast and thereby exposed the forces to unnecessary risk and inefficiency, while others felt they had never worked more efficiently.

Technology-centred military organizations do not necessarily make the forces less dependent on physical relations and geographical location. Distributed systems can be vulnerable too. If an organization becomes very dependent on information and communication systems, this may influence the possibility of operating outside the network grid. Dependence on the technological network carries a great risk that elimination of sensitive parts of the technological system will pacify large parts of the force.

In the Libya case, the key to coordination was that the personnel knew each other and had trained together. Those who communicated best 'at a distance' – outside the local context – were people who already knew each other. If one recalls the person in the situation centre in Oslo who received a phone call from a friend who was offering a place for a Norwegian site survey team on a Belgian plane to Greece the next day, it is apparent that if that call had not happened, the departure would have been delayed, possibly for days. Clearly, operational efficiency is not only dependent on technology but also on human communication and relationships.

Decisions in Networks

In military documents on network-centric warfare, the most important aspects of human cognition are aligned with rational decision theory. The main idea is to integrate technology and humans in order to gather precise information from the whole network to decision-makers (Gomez, 2010). Moreover, the network idea is to protect information with the aid of decentralized storage and alternative distribution channels for information, which is also in line with rational decision theory.

Rational decision-making theory has been called into question since the 1940s (Simon, 1945). Increased amounts of information also mean increased ambiguity (March, Olsen & Christensen, 1976). Decisions emerge in conversations and communication between people who act in power relations with each other, often without being aware of why or how the decisions are made. Simple, linear connections in technology, information, communication, and decisions do not exist in practical reality.

From the Libya case, there is little to support the suggestion that information was made available to the right decision-maker, at least formally speaking. Rather, personnel made direct contact with whom they needed to talk by phone, and these people cooperated and negotiated what they were trying to achieve regardless of others, for example in the matter of the weapons and when the transport plane was 'borrowed' without the involvement of the NJHQ. Moreover, decisions such as when to depart emerged and changed continuously in the conversations between the involved persons.

Communication and Creativity

The hope that the complexity of the world can be tackled by technological superiority assumes that human rationality, and through this communication, can be purified. It is a paradox that while technological and human complexity have increased together with insights of the limitations and contextuality of rationality, the new epiphany for tackling this is a return to pure rationality. The idea of communication in the network-centric warfare concept sustains the traditional communication theory of a sender and a receiver producing uniform meaning in a message conveyed through technological means (Shannon & Weaver, 1949).

There seems to be a notion in modern military strategy that the purpose of communication is to achieve common understanding in situations, and that this will lead to flexibility in operations. The assumption is that communication is a means to achieve a goal and there is a non-complex relation between common understanding and flexibility. At the base of this notion is the idea that the capability to transfer and receive data and information is by itself enough to enable a complete and common understanding of relevant data and information, and by this create a common decontextualized awareness.

Complexity theory implies that these views of communication are unrealistic. The results of the studied case have revealed that the different actors perceived what they experienced in very different ways, despite having the same information. This means that decisions were not taken in the same way in different parts of the distributed activity.

Moreover, different people interpreted the commander's intentions very differently. In fact, the commander's intentions *were* ambiguous. Take just as one example the local logistics officer who went to Crete together with the first crew because he thought it was a matter of urgency, while his commander in Oslo said he could just relax because there was no urgency. Clearly, they had no common understanding of the situation or of the 'commander's intention'.

The common NCW perspective is that collecting information and rapidly putting such information together with precision combat forces and various weapons systems will achieve the desired military effect. The basis for this belief is a linear perception of cause and effects.

In the Libya case, the actors knew little of what kind of weapons they needed most, and they discussed right up until the last moment what types of planes they would offer. They ended up concentrating on F-16s, and at the same time took an assorted sample of weapons, to cover all possible events.

When they left Norway, they had no idea about what would be most effective because decisions about weapons systems and the use of them emerged disconnected from any wider strategic discussion, and with a large degree of uncertainty. Nevertheless, the emerging strategy of the RNoAF turned out to be almost too effective, as their planes, in relative terms, ended up dropping more weapons than any other participating nation.

In the NCW logic, communication is a friction-free flow of information through the organization (the people), which translates information into knowledge in order to achieve full combat efficiency. Through technology, the quality of communication is seen to increase radically, and the risk of misunderstandings, lack of clarity, misinterpretations, and uncertainty will be reduced or even removed entirely.

Not only is communication a means for the strategic leaders to achieve a pre-set goal, but also the professional culture is supposed to contribute to such achievement. Interestingly, military officers are also encouraged to be creative when faced with complexity. In other words, they should come up with solutions that are new and different. Military strategy is often portrayed as more of an art than a science, for example, when references are made to the ancient strategy work *The Art of War* (Sun-tzu, 2011). However, as strategists are also supposed to be completely rational, there seems to be no explanation as to how humans can be completely coordinated and identical in their understanding, while at the same time they can be creative and produce difference.

Complexity, Hierarchy, and Central Control

Traditionally, military strategic thinking has conveyed the message that operational organizations should have one central point where all information is gathered in order to create an overview and control, so that the leaders can make the right decisions. The aim is to uphold the hierarchy and to produce a common situational understanding and awareness. It is the leaders' task to control the central point, which might be operational headquarters, a situation centre, or a strategic central command.

This description of reality is challenged by a complexity view of strategic organization. The idea that hierarchical structures are the most suitable way to make decisions and gain control is less valid in complex and dynamic situations. A large organization consists of a large number of local areas in which tasks are performed relatively independently of each other. Given that these tasks are performed in similar ways (i.e. they are standardized), this should enable recognition and generalization, which in turn have a self-coordinating effect. However, the degree to which the different areas are linked together in the organization is not hierarchical, but the result of direct contact across the distributed areas. Persons in one area talk directly to persons in other areas without going via either a headquarter or a superior leader.

Many such interactions overlap. The conglomerates of interactions are tightly interwoven and complex, but are far from being random. They function as linked local networks. In such non-hierarchical dynamic structures, people construct and interpret information. It is on this basis that we can talk about the emergence of a coordination of *different* understandings that are experienced as *similar*, but never the same. Individual understanding is both uniquely different and similar to other individuals' understanding (Mead, 1934).

During a crisis in which situations develop very rapidly, the hierarchical time horizon will be compressed more than the time taken to sustain formalities in a hierarchy. Sustaining hierarchy as a functional and operational contribution can quite simply take too much time. The headquarters or central command will lag behind because the actions will have already been performed before the information reaches the central command and back again.

In such situations, the decisions about future actions made at the central point will be made after the situation they relate to has occurred. The central operational decisions will then concern the past rather than the future. When this happens, it does not mean that the command centre is rendered without a role, but that its role will differ from that described in emergency plans and official operational organizational designs. It is important to recognize that these complex dynamics exist in operational hierarchies. The hierarchy does not need to be sustained in order to succeed during crises and emergencies.

How Global and Local Strategies Emerge Simultaneously

In the RNoAF's response to the Libyan crisis, the rapid international reaction emerged as a result of negotiations about different intentions and understandings of the situation in many local contexts. The operational reaction meant that for some time local strategies remained unknown to leaders higher up in the formal hierarchy (i.e. leaders who were supposed to take care of strategy).

For example, decisions about what weapons to bring (and ultimately use) were made by phone between operational officers. The decision to transfer a Hercules plane between squadrons was made over a beer in a bar, without informing the operational headquarters in control of the resources. In the local context, such processes might not have seemed to have a wider global strategic impact. However, the types of weapons influenced Norwegian military strategy, because they were indicative of the type of operations the planes could participate in, what role the planes could play in the larger operation, and what military and political consequences it would lead to.

The Norwegian planes ended up being extremely active participants in the Libyan mission. No other country's planes dropped more bombs in proportion to the resources deployed: close to 600 precision weapons were dropped over Libya by Norwegian F-16s.

Emergent Processes

Much of the 'drive' in the work during preparations for the Libyan mission happened as a consequence of meetings between persons discussing face-to-face, by phone, by video conference, and to some extent by text messages and e-mail. In the operations planning group, personnel chose not to make written orders. It became clear how unexpected challenges could be dealt with and solved through conversations between many different actors. Through such communications, an understanding of the structure in the operation emerged at the same time as changes happened. In complexity terms, the mission may therefore be understood as a *process that emerged* in the ongoing interactions between the involved actors.

At the NJHQ, the personnel acknowledged that it was impossible to use the normal planning procedures because it eventually became clear that the time horizon was completely different than in normal exercises and operations that are planned months ahead. The NJHQ personnel had never been through such a preparation process before. Nevertheless, many of the challenges they faced were recognizable to them. Previous planning processes and training had contributed to their preparation for dealing with unforeseen missions. However, experience and training are never any guarantee of success during crisis. The interrelating between all the actors, with all their potential differences, personalities, and ideas of authority and identity responses could have led the operation along a quite different path than it did.

Personal relations were crucial in the preparations for the Libya mission. The importance of knowing each other across formal organizational and geographical boundaries made it much easier to establish contact and to discuss urgent matters. *Trust* between the participants was part of this: they knew and trusted each other's skills and abilities. The actors who were selected for the operational planning group were thought to be the 'right' people. Their relations, experience, and availability were key criteria for their selection.

The collaboration between the RNoAF units and the logistics support unit NDLO resulted from informal personal relations, while formal decisions made higher up in the hierarchy took much longer and were therefore partly bypassed. The administrative procedures, rules, and regulations (bureaucratic practice) had not developed in concert with the idea of the 'rapid response defence organization'. Several of those who participated in the operation claimed that an important reason for the quick response was that it happened during a weekend, while the bureaucrats were away from their offices. By the time the administrators returned to work on Monday morning, the operational organization had already left the country to go to war.

Hence, two quite different organizational patterns existed in tension and shifted in relation with each other with regard to their intentions and understanding of the mission. In peacetime, the operational organization was dominated by the bureaucratic organization's procedures and protocols. As the rapid operational response was called for, the power relation between the two practices shifted immediately. By ascribing this shift to the timing of the event (the weekend), it was made into more or less a coincidence.

However, an alternative understanding could be that there was silent acceptance of a rapid shift of power and organizational priority throughout the hierarchy, all the way up to the Government. Such a silent acceptance of a *spontaneous power shift* in the organization could be the key to understanding the short response time of the deployment.

Time Paradox and Strategy

With respect to departure time and the geographical objective of the deployment, traditional strategy work and procedure would have set the direction and objectives a long time in advance and then worked out a plan for how to achieve the objectives. In the case of the RNoAF's response to the Libyan crisis, there was no concrete information available to the RNoAF about where they were going or what exactly they were going to do. The direction and the objectives were unclear in both a geographical and psychological sense of the words. Some personnel thought it would be weeks before they would leave, then it was 10 days, and then five, before they realized they might leave a couple of days later. While they prepared for the operation, the time of departure kept changing and the time horizon (i.e. the strategy horizon) shrunk.

The strategy for the Norwegian mission to depart on Monday 21 March 2011 emerged in a couple of days and was realized partly without the involvement of central commanders. A crucial part of this development was the access to the Hercules plane on Saturday evening, which enabled 132 LV to send the site survey team to join the Belgians on Sunday, 20 March. The strategic significance of the decision to borrow the Hercules before the NJHQ got hold of it thus related to time. The base where they ended up putting the resources had an impact on the way the resources were used during the operation (i.e. night flights). As part of the large international force, which from the outset was uncoordinated, the arrival time and location of the resources would have an impact on other resources and how they were used in relation to each other by the commanders and at the headquarters.

The strategy was the pattern of action that the commanders were working to make sense of while and after the pattern emerged. Strategy was not only about the *future* but also about the *past*, while it emerged in the *present*. Such circular time paradoxes call for a different meaning of the organizational concept of strategy.

Leadership and Complexity

The Norwegian Joint Headquarters NJHQ was lagging behind in relation to the speed of preparations for deployment. First, they related to 'a few weeks' but later they were prepared to work along a time horizon of 10 days. No general would have ordered them to plan a deployment during a weekend. It seemed that the strategy of rapid deployment came about outside the control of the generals.

In terms of a complexity theoretical description of an organized pattern, it was self-organizing coordination. Self-organization is not a particular technique or prescription akin to the delegation of power or the taking of personal initiatives. It is a description of a fundamental 'social mechanism' of organization, a process whereby human beings interact through communication with other human beings and enact every power and ethical aspect of such interactions.

During the preparations for the Libyan mission, the actors negotiated creative compromises concerning the issue of deploying first and planning later. They convinced and motivated each other to deploy much faster than anyone could imagine. The dynamic was dependent on many people regardless of rank. Some 200 people were willing to work during the weekend on the logistics, 120 people were willing to be deployed, and officers throughout the hierarchy made – or consciously skipped – necessary decisions. Some gained resources based on trust when they 'borrowed' the Hercules, and some confronted a Belgian commanding officer at the Araxos airbase when they thought his style of leadership would jeopardize the deployment.

All of the aforementioned are examples of small actions of power relating with large consequences for the operational strategy, but none of these actions could have been planned, nor were they random. This is the meaning of the term self-organizing processes. It is the interaction of many actors in pursuit of their intentions that produce the structure (i.e. the organization and its strategy as practice).

However, self-organization also means that the result will be highly unpredictable; there is no way to know whether the outcome will be success or failure. Paradoxically, self-organization mostly produces both at the same time, because different actors will experience different outcomes. Different actors will even experience the meaning of the same outcome differently. No major military operation, such as the one to enforce the UN decision on Libya, will ever be just a success or a failure.

Leadership in the Libyan mission was different from what might be seen as the stereotypical understanding of leadership in the Armed Forces. It was not the work of a strong general who, through a clear vision, strategy, and intention, pointed the mission in the right direction. In the mobilization phase, there was an informal tone between officers of different rank; the conversations were calm and constructive, but always with room for disagreement and argument.

One important aspect of that leadership was demonstrated when the commander of the 132 LV, a brigadier general, returned from his holiday the day after the work in the OPG had started under the leadership of a major. The brigadier general did not intervene to take charge merely to signal authority and control. In his mind, that would have ruined the constructive creative work ongoing in the planning group. Instead, he left the major and his group to continue their work and then attended some meetings to show his interest and support but without taking charge, and was otherwise merely briefed by the major.

Hence, the involved actors did not experience the 'strong general' as the performer of leadership, as in the narrative told afterwards by many in the military organization who were not directly involved. When the members of the OPG were asked to identify leadership in their group, they said: 'Leadership grew, emerged, and shifted between a number of people around the table during the meetings. Leadership was in the group, between us. There was not one leader contributing to leadership, we all did'.

In other words, leadership existed 'there and then' in the ongoing interaction processes between the persons involved, when many individuals engaged in driving the group effort forward. Leadership was seen as a social phenomenon. Although there was structure, no one thought of the process in terms of sequential phases. This insight is important in order to understand why the involved actors considered the preparations as a success.

However, if leadership did not belong to one person (the leader), then what role should the leader of the group have had? When the group speeded up the tempo and all leashes were released, the question is whether the formal leader's main role should have been to halt the process and spend some more time reflecting and questioning the mission. Such interference would have disrupted the cohesion, and prevented the group from engaging in groupthink processes.

The brigadier general could have posed more questions to his superiors, since the situation was serious and the Norwegian military was going to fight a war in a remote country without any clear idea on what basis, not to mention the lack of clarity about who was in charge of the international operation. Engaging in quick-fix wars in the Arab world is not the main purpose of Norwegian military forces, and therefore the rather panic-stricken and diffuse statement that the forces had to quickly prevent genocide could have been taken with much more precaution and on the basis of questions such as the following:

What is the real situation in Libya and in what way does this situation relate to any sensible solution that our military forces can provide? What is to be achieved, for what purpose, and for whom? Which one of our allies is asking for military help and which one is not? Is there any critique from allies against this mission, and what are their arguments?

The Norwegian military forces are not supposed to be mobilized on the basis of misunderstandings. GIL, the 132 LV brigadier general, or any of the other involved generals could have declined to mobilize until they had received clear-cut written orders and explanations from the Chief of Defence and the Government in a joint council meeting.

Need for Speed

In reality, 132 LV was released to their own tempo, not very unlike how Delta was released on 22 July. When it comes to very specialized operational groups who spend so much time and effort preparing for scenarios that rarely happen in reality, a leader's role might be to slow them down.

At the time, the 132 LV group seemed to enter a mode of inexplicable hurry to the extent that no one knew why that had happened. Explanations varied from those who thought the rush had been ordered from 'above', to those who thought it had to do with bureaucrats being out of the way because it was the weekend. Some also thought it was just a manifestation of their trained overlearned patterns. In reality, there was no explicit order from above to hurry, and the strategic and operational military leaders would have had the power to slow down the speed.

The explanation of the overlearned patterns seems plausible, given that the group had decided its own speed of response, which in the case of 132 LV meant 'Quick Reaction Alert'. The group thus seemed to split action and reflection: they acted first, and reflected later.

Every military operation is dependent on logistics, a planning-centred activity that could slow down the tempo, given that such operations take a lot of coordination and formalities. In this case, however, there were no 'square-minded' logistics officers who were concerned with having all the papers and formalities in order. Instead, there were creative logistics officers concerned with improvising and making informal and trust-based deals.

On Crete, the logistics team rented a whole hotel for their personnel, without any credit assurances but merely based on trust. Later in the operation, they literally brought a suitcase full of cash from Norway, because the formal electronic credit procedure was not established in the initial phase. At Bodø Air Station, the local NDLO commander engaged heavily in the preparations without any orders from central NDLO commanders.

The engaged logistics officers enabled the extreme speed of the preparations. Their highly local practice is difficult to explain in the language and mantras of traditional strategy planning and organizational leadership. Rather, it is the paradoxical similarities and differences between people in action – the flexibilities and adaptabilities of human behaviour – that carried the dynamics of the network in the preparations for the RNoAF's Libya deployment.

Crisis Behaviour as Cultural Skill

In many ways, 132 LV was thrown into a completely new situation that did not resemble anything they had done in the past. Nevertheless, it appeared as though they had undergone a learning process in the years before the operation, during which they acquired a *cultural skill* that prepared them to act as they did. They could not properly explain where and how they had learned to act exactly as they did. It was not a result of a training programme, but more a result of participation and formation into a professional practice that over time had developed in different local contexts in the RNoAF. The RNoAF is a relatively small and specialized organization in which officers spend many years of their careers. This inevitably brings them into close contact with different people in different parts of the organization, such that many of the officers develop relationships that become highly valuable during a crisis.

Collapse of Operational Leadership

Although the mobilization can be described as a success for the 132 LV, their relations with other units were more of a problem. Many of the officers involved in the mission considered it unacceptable that the NJHQ had lagged behind when the 132 LV started to drive up the tempo of the operation. For the NJHQ, it was likewise not acceptable that 132 LV 'ran off' without the involvement of the NJHQ. The fact that the 132 LV and the NJHQ to some extent operated independently cannot be seen as a success.

Lack of cooperation between the units was a symptom also seen in one of the large exercises that had taken place just before the mission. The RNoAF exercised a coordination of deployment. For some reason, the NJHQ did not participate in this. In a sense, when the Libyan situation emerged, both the RNoAF and the NJHQ did what they had trained for: not collaborating. Inclusion and exclusion processes between the two organizations were an aspect of the power and identity issues they struggled with in their daily work. These processes became a problem when a rapid response was required.

In the bureaucratic practice of AFA, the staff had considerable difficulties in following what was going on, because everything that happened was more relation-based rather than formal. They were very concerned with the fact that they were responsible for the wellbeing of the crews with respect to payment, disability pensions for war injuries, and many other issues.

For example, they were seriously concerned about the insurance coverage for the deployed personnel in cases of injuries or if they were killed in action, because these matters were not clear but rather decided from one mission to the next. In the Libyan operation, they had no time to do this before the first part of the deployment was on its way.

References

Arntzen, A. & Grøtan, T. O. (2011). A new chance for network centric warfare in the context of modernity. In: K. E. Haug & O. L. Maaø (eds). *Conceptualising Modern War*. London: Hurst, pp. 231–257.

Cilliers, P. (2001). Boundaries, hierarchies and networks in complex systems. *International Journal of Innovation Management*, 5(2), pp. 135–147.

Dekker, S., Cilliers, P. & Hofmeyr, J. H. (2011). The complexity of failure: Implications of complexity theory for safety investigations. *Safety Science*, 49(6), pp. 939–945.

Fleming, B. P. (2011). *The Hybrid Threat Concept: Contemporary War, Military Planning and the Advent of Unrestricted Operational Art, Monograph*. Fort Leavenworth, KS: School of Advanced Military Studies.

Gomez, R. M. (2010). *Centralized Command- Decentralized Execution: Implications of Operating in a Network Centric Warfare Environment*. Montgomery, AL: Air War College, Air University.

Hoffman, F. G. (2007). *Conflict in the 21st Century: The Rise of Hybrid Wars*. Arlington, VA: Potomac Institute for Policy Studies Monograph.

Johannessen, S. O. & Stacey, R. D. (2005). Technology as social object: A complex responsive processes perspective. In: R. D. Stacey (ed.). *Experiencing Emergence in Organisations: Local Interaction and the Emergence of Global Pattern*. London: Routledge, pp. 142–163.

March, J. G., Olsen, J. P. & Christensen, S. (1976). *Ambiguity and Choice in Organizations*. Bergen, Norway: Universitetsforlaget.

Mead, G. H. (1934). *Mind, Self and Society*. Chicago: Chicago University Press.

Shannon, C. & Weaver, W. (1949). *The Mathematical Theory of Communication*. Urbana: University of Illinois Press.

Simon, H. (1945). *Administrative Behavior: A Study of Decision-Making Processes in Administrative Organization*. New York: Palgrave Macmillan.

Sun-tzu (2011). *The Art of War*. London: Amber Books Ltd.

11 War Without Strategy
Was It a Success?

The Normalization of War

Since the fall of the Soviet Union in the early 1990s, the Western military alliance NATO, including Norway, for many years saw a shift take place from defence against a well-defined enemy (the Soviet Union) to international operations that would include rapid responses to emerging situations as well as long-term interventions. Examples are the Kosovo intervention in 1999, Afghanistan from 2003 to 2014, Libya in 2011, and the US-led Global Coalition to Counter ISIS (The Islamic State of Iraq and Syria) from 2014.

Also since the 1990s, other global patterns have emerged, such as the development and spread of information and communication networks and media; the globalization of economic trade activities, travel, and tourism on a grand scale; and economic liberalization processes in previously closed totalitarian states, such as Russia and China. More recent developments include the ascendance of authoritarian government, for instance in Turkey, and increased populism and nationalism in the USA – represented by the election of Donald Trump for President in 2016 – and leading European countries, notably UK, France, Germany, and Italy. These developments could be viewed as reactions to almost three decades of global economic and political liberalization. The strategic shift (and thus identity) of the current Western military has emerged as part of these local and global patterns. An example of how this strategic shift emerges as practice is demonstrated in the Libya case.

Deploying Norwegian F-16 fighter planes as part of the NATO operation to deal with the Balkan crisis at the end of the 1990s as opposed to deploying F-16s to enforce the UN's no-fly zone over Libya in 2011 seemed very similar, but they were completely different experiences for the RNoAF personnel, for the military strategic commanders, for the politicians, and for the public.

In the 1990s, deploying Norwegian military and engaging in war outside national borders was a completely new situation that was subject to professional doubt and public debate. Back then, there was a lot of stress involved for the RNoAF in dealing with this new practice of deploying to a very different environment than the one in which they had been trained and were used to operating in. Consequently, they were not mentally prepared. Their mindset, expertise, and practice were oriented towards defending the northern areas of both Norway and NATO against the Soviet Union. However, by 2011, when deploying for war in Libya – far outside Norway's normal sphere of interests – the activities were almost business-as-usual and routine for the RNoAF and the political leaders. In the public domain, a decade of war in Afghanistan seemed to have ended any debate about the deployment of Norwegian military abroad. Going to war had become normalized.

However, in the Libya case some critique was raised against the political decision-making process. Prime Minister Stoltenberg seemed to have taken the decision for Norway to participate in the military operation as part of the preparations for his participation in the Paris meeting on Saturday, 19 March 2011. The formal Government decision was made without a proper meeting with the relevant parliamentary committee and without any public debate in the Norwegian parliament (Stortinget). There is a long-standing tradition in Norway that the opposition parties lie low in matters of foreign and security politics. Politicians are supposed to act united and with outward consensus in such matters. Moreover, the Norwegian Constitution gives the Government a prerogative in matters of national security and foreign policy.

However, the Government carries a democratic responsibility for involving the parliament and for administering a formal decision-making process that reflects accountability. In the Libya case, the Government clearly did not live up to its responsibilities for a formal and democratic discussion before its decision was made to send fighter planes to fight in Libya. It prioritized what it saw as its international responsibilities. No heated debate emerged within Norway because of this. Although Prime Minister Stoltenberg lost the national election in 2013, this was hardly because of the Libya affair. It is more likely that the terrorist attacks four months later played a part. Internationally, however, Stoltenberg's loyalty was appreciated. In 2014, he was appointed Secretary General of NATO.

Was It a Success?

So in what way did the international strategies emerge before, in concert with, and as sensemaking after the military operations? To some extent, the answer to this question becomes clear in the House of Commons Foreign Affairs Committee's investigation into the British role in the Libyan affair. After hearing evidence from key actors and experts, the committee's assessment was that the intervention had lacked intelligence to back up claims from the politicians that they needed to act fast because Gaddafi's army were posing a threat to civilians. The operation was later criticized for changing its objective from establishing a no-fly zone and protecting civilians against non-proportional Libyan army action to ending Colonel Gaddafi's regime by exterminating much of his military capabilities and attempting to assassinate him:

> Many Western policymakers genuinely believed that Muammar Gaddafi would have ordered his troops to massacre civilians in Benghazi, if those forces had been able to enter the city. However, while Muammar Gaddafi certainly threatened violence against those who took up arms against his rule, this did not necessarily translate into a threat to everyone in Benghazi. In short, the scale of the threat to civilians was presented with unjustified certainty. US intelligence officials reportedly described the intervention as 'an intelligence-light decision' . . . . We have seen no evidence that the UK Government carried out a proper analysis of the nature of the rebellion in Libya. It may be that the UK Government was unable to analyse the nature of the rebellion in Libya due to incomplete intelligence and insufficient institutional insight and that it was caught up in events as they developed. It could not verify the actual threat to civilians posed by the Gaddafi regime; it selectively took elements of Muammar Gaddafi's rhetoric at face value; and it failed to identify the militant Islamist extremist element in the rebellion. The UK strategy was founded on erroneous assumptions and an incomplete understanding of the evidence.
>
> (House of Commons Foreign Affairs Committee,
> 2016a, HC119, p. 15)

In reality, the operation's drift towards a regime change was a result of an interpretation of the resolution's 'all necessary measures' element:

> The United States was instrumental in extending the terms of Resolution 1973 beyond the imposition of a no-fly zone to include the authorisation of 'all necessary measures' to protect civilians. In practice, this led to the imposition of a 'no-drive zone' and the assumed authority to attack the entire Libyan Government command and communications network.
>
> (House of Commons Foreign Affairs Committee,
> 2016a, HC119, p. 12)

The British Secretary of Defence at the time of the Libyan crisis, Dr Liam Fox, testified before the Committee that:

> The view was taken that the UN resolution said to take all possible measures to protect civilians, and that meant a constant degradation of command and control across the country. That meant not just in the east of the country, but in Tripoli.
>
> (House of Commons Foreign Affairs Committee,
> 2016b, HC 520, Q156)

The changed understanding of the operation from the UN resolution's 'all necessary measures', to the UK Government's interpretation 'all possible measures' made a significant difference when it came to practical action for the Norwegian part of the operation. On the night of 25 April 2011, two Norwegian F-16s bombed Gaddafi's residence in Tripoli, an incident that would be inconceivable a few weeks earlier. The attack legitimized the killing of Gaddafi and hence, a regime change. By dropping almost 600 bombs, the Norwegian mission did what was *possible*, not what was *necessary* for them to do.

Regarding the risk of a massacre in Benghazi, expert witnesses Alison Pargeter and Professor George Joffé stated (House of Commons Foreign Affairs Committee, 2016b, HC520, Q1):

> I don't see evidence of some large-scale massacre of civilians in Benghazi.
>
> (Alison Pargeter)

> I don't really think there was any danger of the kind of massacre of civilians that was suggested at the time.
>
> (Professor George Joffé)

Instead of providing evidence to back up the intervention decision, the power interaction of different actor's intentions had driven the development of the situation. As for strategy, the Committee's view that 'the UK strategy was founded on erroneous assumptions and an incomplete understanding of the evidence' (HCFAC, 2016a, HC119, p. 15) was opposed by Lord Hague of Richmond, the UK's Foreign Secretary at the time of the Libyan crisis, who said the following about the discussion in the UK's National Security Council (NSC): 'We all had a good understanding of where we were and what the strategy was' (HCFAC, 2016b, HC 520, Q170). Lord Hague was talking about the political strategy before the UN resolution was passed. It seems that the UK Government intended to carve out a resolution, which it could later rely on to justify its actions towards a regime change. Lord Hague of Richmond stated:

> Indeed, the decision to intervene if a UN resolution could be passed was taken at a meeting of the NSC. This truly was the end of sofa Government in these matters. The decision was taken in the NSC with all relevant people present, and I remember the Prime Minister summing up the meeting and saying, 'The key question is this: is it in the British national interest, if this is about to happen in Benghazi and this conflict is happening in this way, for us to intervene? That is the question we have to decide.' And having taken opinions from all around the room, he concluded that it was. So that was specifically the terms of the NSC decision.
>
> (House of Commons Foreign Affairs Committee, 2016b, HC 520, Q171)

At the meeting in Paris on 19 March 2011, the political decision-makers, including the Norwegian Prime Minister, seem to have been aware of the fact that they were going for a regime change and legitimizing it by changing their understanding of the resolution from 'all necessary measures' to 'all possible measures'. Not all parts of the UN's resolution were regarded as equally important. The resolution also stated that there should be a strict implementation of the arms embargo, yet the international community turned a blind eye on this part, since the French and others supported the provision of arms to rebel groups. Consequently, the primary objective of the intervention changed from protecting the people of Benghazi to broad participation in the rebel war to end the Gaddafi regime:

> The combination of coalition airpower with the supply of arms, intelligence and personnel to the rebels guaranteed the military defeat of the Gaddafi regime. On 20 March 2011, for example, Muammar Gaddafi's forces retreated some 40 miles from Benghazi following attacks by French aircraft. If the primary object of the coalition intervention was the urgent need to protect civilians in Benghazi, then this objective was achieved in less than 24 hours.
>
> (House of Commons Foreign Affairs Committee, 2016a, HC119, p. 17)

While politicians seemed to wage military power on a rather thin foundation, voices from the military expressed concern. The Committee asked the UK Chief of the Defence Staff at the time of the Libyan crisis, Lord Richards, whether the object of British policy in Libya was civilian protection or regime change. He responded that 'one thing morphed almost ineluctably into the other' as the campaign developed its own momentum. He had expressed his concern about the strategic direction of the March 2011 campaign:

> During Benghazi, an increasingly influential set of people started saying, 'If we're really going to protect civilians, you've got to get rid of Gaddafi.' That is when I said, 'Well, is that really sensible? What are we going to do if he goes?' and all the things that I had learned through bitter experience. That was rather ignored in the majority view, which was, 'We need to get rid of him, simply to make sure we meet the political aim of preventing large-scale civilian loss of life.'
>
> (House of Commons Foreign Affairs Committee, 2016a, HC119, p. 17)

The Committee commented on the democratic process in the case of Britain:

> When Prime Minister David Cameron sought and received parliamentary approval for military intervention in Libya on 21 March 2011,

he assured the House of Commons that the object of the intervention was not regime change. In April 2011, however, he signed a joint letter with United States President Barack Obama and French President Nicolas Sarkozy setting out their collective pursuit of 'a future without Gaddafi.'

(House of Commons Foreign Affairs Committee,
2016a, HC119, p. 18)

The Norwegian Prime Minister, Stoltenberg, avoided a similar critique, because he had made the decision to use Norwegian military forces in Libya without public debate in the Norwegian parliament (Stortinget). However, there is no evidence to suggest that he did not fully share the UK Government's intentions of a regime change. The Committee's critique of UK policy would therefore be equally valid as a critique against the glide of strategic objectives in the Norwegian military involvement in Libya:

> The UK's intervention in Libya was reactive and did not comprise action in pursuit of a strategic objective. This meant that a limited intervention to protect civilians drifted into a policy of regime change by military means.

(House of Commons Foreign Affairs Committee,
2016a, HC119, p. 18)

In relation to mainstream strategy theory, this conclusion clearly shows how reality in the Libyan affair evolved very differently from such theory. This realization is also the basis of a complexity theoretical critique against mainstream theory. In dynamical and rapidly emerging situations, organizations such as the military do not make strategies as planned actions to obtain strategic objectives in the long-term future. Strategies rather emerge as a response to a rapidly emerging and changing reality, both on a small (local) and large (global) scale at the same time. The decision-makers might give the impression that they are in control. However, as the case shows, those in power are no more in control than anyone else. When faced with rapid change, their responses are just as uninformed, intuitive, political, and above all, local, as those of any group in the response matrix.

The UK Government's National Security Council was a small group in London, UK. The 132 LV operational planning group was a small group in Bodø, Norway. Both these groups, and many others, totally independent and disconnected in the network of power actors, influenced the emergence of the strategy in the Libya operation. This is what I mean by local and global strategies emerging simultaneously and unpredictably.

Strategic Complexity Becomes Strategic Simplicity

There was no coordinated international strategy when the mobilization for the operation in Libya started. For the commanders, there were no pre-planned strategies. They had to relate to a fuzzy UN objective and to different political objectives by different countries' leaders. They also had to relate to the enormous military force, which rapidly, but in an uncoordinated manner, rallied in various places around the Mediterranean. The operation did not become a NATO operation until 29 March, when Canadian Lieutenant General Charles Bouchard was appointed commander of the joint NATO forces.

In a lecture delivered at the RNoAF Academy in March 2012, Bouchard recalled that at the outset of his mission he had used the large NATO operations manual as a doorstop because he considered it useless as a reference for procedure and that it was better to use it to keep the door open for anyone who wanted to bring ideas to him. Clearly, any strategy for the operation emerged after the operation had started. The traditional idea of strategy before action was replaced with action before strategy.

Drawing on complexity theory, the processes of emerging strategies can be described as self-organizing processes. Such processes produce both structured and unstructured human actions as human actions produce the processes. These processes are not controlled by anyone, even if they produce organized patterns and, in hindsight, seem coordinated and controlled.

Military personnel who were not part of the operation later spoke informally about what they thought might be the reason for the successful deployment of the RNoAF to the Libyan operation. One could hear them speak of how well planned they thought the operation was and how the success clearly depended upon the leadership of a strong general. This narrative was far from the story told by those involved, for whom the strategic route was a process that was mostly unplanned and unknown. There were no clear plans and no strong general to lead them at the local level in Bodø, at the national level in Oslo, or at the international level in NATO.

In this situation, the decision in the lower ranks of the RNoAF to bring 'the whole package' of weapons and to deploy to a base that could support night flights clarified a fluid strategic situation as a very simple one for the Royal Norwegian Air Force: to protect civilian Libyans against Libyan army attacks meant bombing any Libyan military capability, including its commander-in-chief Colonel Gaddafi.

References

House of Commons Foreign Affairs Committee (2016a). Libya: Examination of Intervention and Collapse and the UK's Future Policy Options. Third Report of Sessions 2016–17. Report HC119. London: House of Commons.

House of Commons Foreign Affairs Committee (2016b). Libya: Examination of intervention and Collapse and the UKs Future Policy Options, Report HC 520. London: House of Commons.

Part IV

Comparisons and Conclusions

12 Police and Military Cases Compared

Organizational Practices

The purpose of the last part of this book is to compare some of the aspects of the two cases presented and discussed in the previous parts. I discuss the similarities and contrasts in the two cases, and present some new ideas that help to explain these similarities and contrasts.

First, the two cases are compared with a view to organizational practices, and then in the next chapter the cases are compared with regard to strategy. The final chapter structures the main conclusions to be drawn from this study.

Organizational Practices

In the context of the two cases, there are two major organizational practices in the police and the military: the operational and the bureaucratic. In the following, I focus attention on the differences between the two practices and the direct impact of the differences in the specific events. I will refer to the respective operational practices of the two organizations as the *police operational practice* and the *military operational practice*. With respect to bureaucratic practices, I differentiate between two types of bureaucratic practice: *juridical-bureaucratic practice* and *political-bureaucratic practice*. The former is the practice of professional operational bureaucracies, a practice in which laws and regulations guide the administrative activity. By contrast, the political-bureaucratic practice is a practice whereby bureaucracy interacts with, and acts on behalf of, government politicians in order to implement political initiatives and influence the management of professional operational bureaucracies, which in the studied cases are the police and the military.

The Boundaries Between Bureaucratic and Operational Practices

In the 22 July case, a terrorist attack mobilized the need for the leaders in the dominantly bureaucratic practice in the National Police Directorate (POD) to collaborate more closely with the leaders in the operational practice in Oslo Police District (Oslo PD) and North Buskerud Police District

(NBPD). The reason was that they needed the hierarchy to be intact during the emergency. The hierarchy separates the bureaucratic practice and the operational practice quite distinctively at particular levels, and in the case of the Norwegian police this separation level is between the district's police chiefs and the leaders of the National Police Directorate. Therefore, for the police hierarchy to function well, POD's leaders and the police chiefs had to collaborate.

On 22 July 2011, however, some of the key operational leaders directed their attention downwards in the hierarchy, away from the operational-bureaucratic boundary and towards the tactical operation, while key leaders in POD directed their attention upwards in the hierarchy, away from the same boundary towards the politicians and the political bureaucracy. This left a leadership vacuum in the hierarchical zone between the bureaucratic and operational practices. As a result, hierarchical leadership collapsed not only within the bureaucratic practices, but also within the operational practices (e.g. between NBPD and Delta).

The political-bureaucratic practice dominates military operational practice in peacetime. In the Libya case, political practitioners were flexible during the crisis and operated in a collaboration zone between the military operational and the political-bureaucratic practices. Leadership was sustained under pressure because politicians and military practitioners maintained close contact. Military operational practitioners were more flexible in performing leadership and ran fewer risks in the boundary zone between the operational and bureaucratic practices. Consequently, the hierarchy was sustained in an important way, at least at the strategic and political levels. The key persons had a chance of being involved, even if there are unanswered questions of how they managed their involvement.

Group Identity

In the police case, the two first officers on the quay opposite the island (P30A and P30B) were criticized by the 22 July Commission for not going to Utøya immediately after their arrival at the quay. It is not known whether they considered or discussed the possibility of going to the island. The Commission's report does not indicate that there was any disagreement between the two officers during the operation. Moreover, it is not known whether this means that they aligned their explanations, whether any discrepancies were smoothed out by the official inquiry, or whether they agreed early on not to go to Utøya.

However, it *is* known that the two officers split up; one went down to the adjacent quay and the other later went to the main road to meet Delta. The former officer helped people off an incoming boat, but later denied having seen the boat. If his behaviour reflected operational police group identity, it would make sense that he did not want to use that boat alone or even with his partner, but rather would have thought about helping the people who came ashore from the boat.

Helping to rescue people would be in line with normal individual actions in the police operational group practice, but going to the island to kill or arrest one or more terrorists would not have been in accordance with normal practice. However, in the eyes of the law a police officer's loyalty to his or her group cannot be used as an excuse for not acting individually. On the contrary, as pointed out by the Commission, the law clearly says that police officers are individually duty-bound to interfere to prevent or stop ongoing criminal activity.

The police officer who claimed he did not remember having seen the boat right next to him could very well have been in a state of shock or panic, and he might even have suffered a memory loss as a consequence, but it is also likely that the explanation he gave to the Commission was one that best fitted with his understanding of the priorities of his organization's operational practice, namely that the operational group had first priority. Hence, opting to stay and not go to the island was *a normal act*, while the opposite would have been an act outside the normal identity of the police operational group.

Also for the Emergency Response Unit (Delta), the group identity was the main organizational aspect. The members of Delta did everything they could to avoid splitting their group. Their mission was much clearer than that of the two officers on the quay. Delta needed to go to the island and arrest or kill the terrorist or terrorists. To do this, they had to work as a group. This meant that they needed to agree on the rally point. However, when they reached the mainland area opposite the island, they dispersed. One car went to the camping site, one drove past it and ended at Elstangen, and the four cars behind the first two stopped at the main road above Utøya mainland quay. It is not known why the four units did not attempt to cross to the island from the first rally point.

What *is* known is that the other two Delta units were at different sites. One of them returned to Utøya mainland quay, thus making a joint group of five units, but one unit was still left on Elstangen. The group of five chose to join the unit on Elstangen. Thus, the fact remains that, at the moment Delta decided to go to Utøya, the most visible characteristics of the group was the units' eagerness to stick together and work as one group. When the NBPD's rubber boat emerged at Elstangen, this created a problem for the group because all members wanted to enter the boat and they ended up overloading it. Later, their rational explanation suggested that they were not sure how many terrorists there were. A less rational explanation, regarded even by the Commission as a fact, was that the group was overly eager to act as a group.

My analysis of the case suggests that leadership of the group failed considerably. In the situation in which the whole group could not stick together, and faced with the grim prospect that this might be the last time they would see their colleagues, a leader's job should have been to interfere and separate them into smaller and more efficient groups.

A similar kind of group identity exists in the military operational practice in the Libya case. The various smaller units acted out of loyalty to their local group over the larger group and hierarchy. The mission was not controlled by the Norwegian Joint Headquarters (NJHQ), but was propelled by the QRA unit 132 LV in Bodø.

Although not in the same sense as Delta, the F-16 pilots are also part of an elite group in the Armed Forces. The similarity has to do with how they are trained to react. The particular QRA pilots are on 15 minutes' alert, and trained to react to an immediate threat. Their daily work on behalf of the Western alliance of NATO is to identify and intercept Russian flights along the Norwegian coast. The 132 LV is an active border patrol between the West and Russia. International relations are dependent on the pilots' skills and judgements in close encounter with their Russian counterparts. To call on 132 LV is to call on immediate reaction. When the 132 LV learned that it probably would be ordered to fly to Libya, it immediately started to prepare for the mission, with no hesitation and few questions asked. However, like Delta, they too prioritized speed at the expense of alignment and coordination. Hence, they were pushing the organization they were dependent on to the brink of collapse.

Norms

The rule-driven juridical bureaucracy collapsed in both cases. They were just too slow to respond, and their time loss drew them in the opposite direction of the operational practitioners.

The political bureaucrats in the two cases (i.e. those working for the Ministry of Justice and the Ministry of Defence) acted differently, partly due to the different ways they are formally organized. The Chief of Defence is integrated with the Ministry of Defence, allowing for very quick interactions between the military and the political leadership, whereas in the police, the National Police Commander is not integrated with the Ministry of Justice in such a way that allows for immediate interaction. On 22 July 2011, the Minister of Justice did not even know who the National Police Commander was at the time.

The confusion was compounded by the fact that the Ministry of Justice had been hit during the bomb attack. The politicians reacted very much on individual basis, seeking to gain control, but most of all they wanted information and pursued it wherever they could, even if it meant interfering with the work of the operational leaders. Prime Minister Jens Stoltenberg, for example, was mainly concerned with how the situation would appear politically. Officially, he and his advisors later admitted that it was most important to appear to be in control when leaders from other countries called.

Stoltenberg must have been worried about the fact that the Prime Minister's office had been blown away while he was responsible for national security, and even more worried when he learned that the terrorist was attacking his own party's youth summer camp on Utøya. He wanted information fast, not only in his role as Prime Minister but also for very personal reasons. However, during the whole of the evening of 22 July, the operational leaders were unable to give him any reliable information.

Among the juridical-bureaucratic practitioners (i.e. in POD), senior leaders prioritized in accordance with the rules and tried to uphold the hierarchy by directing their attention 'upwards' in the hierarchy. POD's acting leader was mainly interested in the Government's Crisis Council and the Prime Minister's requests, but he was in fact responsible for coordination and leadership 'downwards' in the operational practice.

However, lower in the hierarchy, the operational and tactical leaders were not upholding the hierarchy. The chief of police in Oslo PD did not make contact with his superiors in POD.

In the military case, the hierarchy also collapsed, although in a different way. Prime Minister Stoltenberg and the Minister of Defence primarily operated within their own practice. The location of the Armed Forces situation centre (Sitsen) made it possible for the Minister of Defence and the Chief of Defence to stop by and acquire quick updates without any interference with the operational coordination work. Sitsen officers and other officers at the strategic level bypassed the operational level of the defence organization and exchanged information directly with the tactical units. The message from GIL to 132 LV was to move as fast as possible without worrying about budgets or other administrative personnel rules and routines; his signal was 'deploy first, plan later'.

GIL's role is an interesting example of both strategic and tactical leadership at the same time. In peacetime, his role as Commander of the Air Force is clearly part of the strategic leadership of the Armed Forces. However, in operations, he hands over command of his forces to the operational command at the NJHQ, NATO, or other command structures approved by the Government and Chief of Defence. In the very rapid mobilization during the weekend in March 2011, he provided both strategic and tactical leadership, but that depended on bypassing the operational level at the NJHQ and the internal military bureaucracy.

Communication and Time Elasticity

The communication patterns of the juridical-bureaucratic practices were similar in the police case and the military case. The practitioners wanted to communicate in writing and follow procedure, which generally led to time loss. In the police case, this had negative effects on the police operation at crucial moments.

The national alarm, which should have been sent out by Kripos, took 40 minutes to process because the operator was preoccupied with procedure. Those minutes came on top of the 40 minutes that Oslo PD's operations centre used to notify Kripos. By the time the national alarm was out, the terrorist had managed to escape and reach the ferry quay on the mainland opposite Utøya. As a national special investigation unit, Kripos operated according to juridical-bureaucratic routine.

This was also the case for the Oslo PD operational staff and to some extent also their operations centre. In accordance with juridical-bureaucratic practice, they were required to log all information. However, they were in the midst of an operational practice in which they were dependent on oral information exchange and group cooperation to speed up the response. The 40-minute delay in transmitting the information about the terrorist's escape van is an example of the tension between operational and bureaucratic practices amid the disarray. How did this happen?

Because the emergency phone services at the operations centre were overloaded, incoming phone calls were routed to the ordinary phone service of Oslo PD. There, overwhelmed by information, one of the civilian operators managed to act on a very important message. Near the bombed area, one witness had seen a grey van leaving soon before the explosion. The witness thought it strange because the driver was wearing a police uniform and carrying a gun but left in an unmarked van. The observant witness had made a note of the car's registration number. The phone service operator considered this information so important that she left her desk with the information on a note, walked to the operations centre, and handed the note to the operations leader while briefing her about why she (the operator) thought it was important.

The leader of the operations centre put the note on a desk in the operations room and it was left there for 40 minutes before it was spotted by an operator and forwarded to Kripos. By leaving the note and at the same time briefing the operations leader, the phone service operator acted simultaneously in an operational and a bureaucratic practice. The operational leader then chose to react bureaucratically by placing the note on the desk of a stressed operator in the operations centre, without an oral brief. Unlike the bureaucratic practice, which favours written communication, oral communication is the primary way of communicating and sharing knowledge in operational practices.

From the moment when the operations leader chose bureaucratic practice over operational practice, this seemingly small detail rippled non-linearly through the time horizon. The result was that the opportunity for the police to stop the terrorist leaving Oslo on his way to his next target was lost.

It is evident from the 22 July Commission's report that the operations leader was stressed. Her ability to process complex and multiple information streams was probably reduced. If so, the selection of information and the power relations by which information was selected would have been crucial. It raises the question: was the information deemed less important by the operations leader because it was selected by a civilian phone service operator and not by a police officer?

In the military case, written orders were processed after the actions had taken place. The logistics officer who joined the site survey team from Bodø to Greece received his orders three weeks later. Staff at the NJHQ adhered to procedure more than the tactical groups in Bodø and elsewhere: they followed a juridical-bureaucratic practice. Throughout the process, the NJHQ was constantly asking for updates on what had already happened, without being able to influence what was going to happen.

Procedure would mean at least 28 days for preparation. Judging from orders going in and out of the NJHQ, it is clear that the NJHQ was ready to accept 10 days to deployment. The difference in time horizons between the NJHQ and 132 LV might be explained if their activities are viewed as embedded in different organizational communication practices. The communication practice of the tactical unit 132 LV was oral and group-oriented (operational practice), which compressed (speeded up) the time horizon. The communication practice of the operational headquarters was formal, individualized, and in text (juridical-bureaucratic practice), which expanded (slowed down) the time horizon.

Power and Ethics

Power relations differed in the two cases. In the police operational practice, power was embedded in and between various operational groups and individuals. As mentioned above, in the Oslo PD, just after the bomb blast there was hectic activity at the operations centre, but the staff there did not succeed in sharing critical information about the terrorist's van.

However, from the Commission's report it is clear that the Oslo PD operations centre was excluded from their designated role as a result of the internal power dynamics. The female operations leader was bypassed by both the incident commander on the ground and the operational staff, and hence rendered incompetent.

In the critical hour after the bomb blast, the experienced male incident commander did not talk to his superior commander (i.e. the inexperienced female operations leader) but he did talk and exchange tactical information directly with another experienced male incident commander who had volunteered for the operational function within the operational staff. The local operational chain of command is as follows: the incident commander reports to the leader of the operations centre, who reports to the leader of the operational staff. The operations centre coordinates tactical information, which in the studied case included vital witness information concerning the terrorist's escape van.

The experienced incident commander who suddenly was a member of the operational staff had no experience of such work. He ignored that the operational staff should communicate with the operations leader, not with the incident commander on the ground. However, he knew the incident commander on the ground. Clearly, bypassing the operations leader was a result of the two men knowing and trusting each other's experience more than they trusted the operations leader. They probably communicated very well and thought they did what was best, but they did not seem to realize that bypassing the operations centre's effort to coordinate information would make it more difficult to stop the terrorist.

In NBPD, the situation was similar regarding the relations between the operations centre and the officers on the ground. Various officers acted, but they also waited for orders from the operations centre, such as in the case of the rally point information. Almost 45 minutes after the initial call to NBPD concerning the shootings on Utøya, there still was confusion within NBPD's tactical forces about where they should meet.

There were also power issues between Delta, NBPD's tactical force, and NBPD's operations centre. Delta insisted that NBPD's operations centre had decided the rally point, because it fell under their responsibility. At the same time, the operations centre accepted and assumed that Delta had made the decision. Other police officers also looked to Delta for a decision on the rally point, despite the fact that Delta was not formally participating in the operation. The 22 July Commission called the decision to change the rally point a 'misunderstanding', but it was more the result of a power issue between the various groups.

There were power issues between the smaller NBPD and the larger Oslo PD. A tactical commander in the Oslo PD's operational staff called the chief of police in NBPD and insisted/ordered that she got her operational staff organized. The chief of NBPD later complained to the 22 July Commission that although Oslo PD had sent Delta, she had not formally requested this. Thus, the *ordinary* police operational practice represented a *time expansion* (i.e. passivity), while in the *special* police operational practice of Delta there was *time compression* (i.e. hyperactivity). When Delta came into contact with the local police and needed coordination, their initial time gain was transformed into time loss.

The power issues were clearer in the police than in the military. The operations planning group (OPG) did not wait for the chief of 132 LV, who arrived one day after the OPG had started to work on the Libya plan; he told the OPG to carry on. The Inspector General of the Air Force (GIL) left the tactical unit 132 LV to decide how fast they could deploy, which clearly was an operational decision, not to say a strategic one. With regard to weapons and administrative details, 132 LV acted outside any clear operational or strategic discussion with their superiors. The unit even 'stole' a Hercules transport plane in the process.

In the Libya case, there was a time expansion within the bureaucratic practice. This practice quickly collapsed and became obsolete as the political practice compressed in time until it collapsed in terms of strategic coordination. Who were most eager for war, the politicians or the military? It was clearly the politicians, but the generals did not seem to have any objections that would stagger the politicians' appetite for military action. The Chief of Defence's only concern seemed to be command of the forces, but he did not insist on having more solid strategic ground before sending forces on a mission to Libya.

Although the entire power dynamics in the military was one of more flexibility and non-hierarchical network dynamics compared with the police, it is worth noting that this flexibility in power relations between political and military top leaders also undermined any thorough discussion and analysis of the situation.

The Libya case thus reveals a very problematic lack of formal structure in the strategic decision process concerning the use of military forces. In Norway, there is no national security council where the politicians and military leaders can meet. Moreover, within the military, there is no formalized top strategic council where the military leaders can meet together with experts to discuss what is known and what is not known about the situation into which they are considering intervening with military action. Consequently, when the politicians speeded up the decision-making process, the military strategists were unable to provide any solid and competent strategic advice to the politicians.

In the Libya case, the decision-making process had the advantage of flexibility in crisis, but it had a remarkable drawback of being so fragmented that it brought the decision-making to the brink of collapse and incompetence. Every serious aspect of the Libya intervention was made clear in retrospect, almost none in prospect. A structured decision-making process might not have changed the decision to contribute with F-16s to the international operation, but at least it would have made it clear who argued what on which basis, thus holding decision-makers accountable for their decisions. On the UK side, we saw how the House of Commons inquiry made public how the political and military leaders reasoned in the decision-making process. In Norway, this is still in the dark.

Enactment

Thus far, in the context of national emergency and international crisis, I have discussed the organizational practices of the Norwegian police and military in terms of communication, power, identity, and ethics, which are formulations of social objects: generalized and particularized social behaviour. The idea of social objects also has something in common with Weick's idea of *enactment*:

> The term 'enactment' is used to preserve the central point that when people act, they bring events and structures into existence and set them in motion. People who act in organizations often produce structures,

constraints, and opportunities that were not there before they took action. Enactment involves a process, enactment, and a product, an enacted environment.

(Weick, 1988, pp. 306–307)

In the following chapter, I will pursue this further in a discussion of strategy.

Reference

Weick, K. E. (1988). Enacted sense making in crisis situations. *Journal of Management Studies*, 25(4), pp. 305–317.

13 Police and Military Cases Compared

Strategy

Non-linearity and Scale in Strategic Response to Crisis and Emergency

When the coalition of predominantly Western countries, including Norway, reacted very quickly to the emerging Libyan crisis, the action was justified on the grounds of what might otherwise have happened had they instead waited. The winning argument was that the coalition could contain the danger by acting quickly. Sensible as this may have seemed, the problem was that the reaction itself was not contained or controllable. It was rolled out on such a large scale and so rapidly that it was impossible for the involved actors to think about the ramifications of what they were doing. No one in the RNoAF did know beforehand that they were going to drop almost 600 bombs, let alone how they would limit those drops to the objective of stopping attacks on civilians in an emerging civil war in Libya without engaging in regime change.

When it comes to crisis management, it is important to take account of paradox and non-linearity. In the Libya case, non-linear escalation did not just work in the direction that the coalition was trying to stop, that of violence and violent rhetoric against civilians in Libya. The intervention itself was also non-linear, and created new escalations that were impossible to stop. After the airstrikes had stopped, a new situation had emerged, this time in the form of continued civil war.

The Uppsala Conflict Data Program (2016), a public data resource that includes information on different types of organized violence (e.g. actors involved, casualties, date, and location), reported that between 152 and 168 civilians were deliberately killed by the pro-Gaddafi forces in 2011, while between 1914 and 3466 people were killed during the fighting in 2011.

When organizational processes escalate, leaders have important roles in slowing down the speed of events, but they can only slow down those parts into which they are coupled. Delta could have slowed down its units' tempo to make sense of the complexity of the situation, but this would have risked more killings by the terrorist. The politicians and generals could have slowed down the speed of the mobilization of international forces, but they would have risked not stopping escalations of the attacks on Libyan civilians. However, the international intervention also enabled the conditions in which the continued civil war could emerge. In some sense, RNoAF and the international forces constructed the very conditions within which they acted.

Action intervenes in the causes of further actions and responses, and thus constructs the next phase of action and the response to it. The next phase is unpredictable, because it is dependent not only on the action of one actor but also on the multiple actions and responses from many other actors, none of whom have control over all the others. In an emerging situation that escalates into the unknown, a reaction that is set in motion to prevent a particular outcome will itself influence the conditions for the outcome that it is meant to prevent. In the Libya situation, the international action escalated into a pathway of the event universe that aided and provided energy for new situations that were just as unwanted as those that the military action was set out to prevent. In the wake of the NATO intervention, Libya disintegrated even more.

This is a reminder – in the age of rapid response – of the importance of having a broader discussion before setting in motion large-scale military actions. It is also really a reminder of taking seriously strategy in the traditional sense of the word – taking account of rationality and analysis.

Local and National Emergency

In the 22 July case, the reality of strategic rationality and analysis was lost sight of the moment the bureaucratic leaders were thrown into an operational practice. They had great difficulties converting into operational practice the very decisions they had taken when they were in their normal bureaucratic practice.

In a *national emergency response*, the Ministry of Justice is defined as the strategic level, whereas the chief of police in a police district is defined as the strategic leader in a *local emergency response*. In the case of the terrorist bomb attack against Government buildings, the incident clearly was local and within Oslo PD, whereas the target, the symbolism, and the ramifications were national.

Hence, there was a big difference as to whether the emergency on 22 July 2011 was immediately perceived by a number of leaders in the hierarchy to be local or national. The linear hierarchy and models in POD's preparedness manual had not taken into consideration the possibility that an emergency could be both local and national.

On 22 July 2011, there was a lot of confusion about the 'levels' and what they meant for practical action. The fact that formal manuals only described ideal situations was a major shortcoming. The manuals did not describe the realities of dynamic and chaotic events.

In practice, *operational leadership* and *operational decision-making* in a national emergency deals with the coordination of decisions across a number of units and districts concerning the use of resources that one district (in the studied case, Oslo PD or NBPD) does not control alone. According to its manual, POD's first priority on 22 July should have been to coordinate the operational resources. Strategic decisions in such a situation could be to ask for military assistance or to approve resources beyond or across usual budget areas. The ministry in charge of responding to the emergency (the Ministry of Justice) had the authority to make such decisions. However, on 22 July 2011, the Ministry of Justice was in ruins because of the bomb.

When an incident is *not national*, the local police district's operational staff make 'strategic decisions'. Such decisions include coordinating the local district's internal resources and taking precautionary safety measures against the spreading effects of the incident by, for example, closing off and securing areas, evacuating people, or requesting assistance from neighbouring districts.

In the case of Oslo PD's chief of police, it seemed unclear what kind of decisions he was responsible for after the bomb exploded. When the 22 July Commission asked him whether he took any *strategic decisions*, he confirmed that he had done so and emphasized decisions about first aid, saving lives, and securing members of the royal family and the political leaders of the country. Other such decisions included that people should leave central Oslo and that public transport services should continue to operate as normal. He was talking about strategic decisions in the local context, while in reality, by requesting a national alarm, he had already defined the situation as a national emergency and his decisions as tactical.

During the 22 July Commission's inquiry several months after the event, both the Commission and the top leader of Oslo PD still clearly thought he had strategic responsibility in the event. This might explain why the Oslo PD's chief of police did not cooperate well with POD and the Ministry of Justice on the strategic and operational issues that emerged during the events on 22 July.

Regarding the security of the royal family and the Government, Crown Prince Haakon was in southern Norway and was not made aware what had happened in Oslo by his personal security detail (PSD) until more than half an hour after the bomb had exploded. The royal family's PSD are part of Oslo PD. They were not informed about the bomb, nor were they told to enhance security for the Crown Prince. Rather, the PSD officers got their information from the Internet and had to improvise based on their own understanding of the incident.

Several members of the Government, including the Minister of Justice, were without any police protection for a long time after the bomb had exploded. The Minister of Justice was on his way by car to his summer holiday home, 400 km from Oslo. He got in touch with a local police officer when he heard the news from Oslo.

In the deep forests of Norway, the scene was far from the manuals of terror response. At the roadside, a local police officer suddenly found himself with the Minister of Justice, discussing what to do after terrorism had blown up the minister's offices and large parts of the Government complex. They decided that the best solution for the minister was that the police officer drove him to Oslo. Thus, when the country was hit by the most violent attack since World War II, the threat assessment and security of the minister in charge of internal security was not made by Oslo PD or the Norwegian Police Security Service, but in a conversation between the minister and a rural police officer in a forest 400 km from Oslo. One may ask on behalf of the local police officer: Was it a local or a national emergency for him?

Operational Network Strategies in the Two Cases

Disruptions as Initiators of Network Strategies

In the 22 July case, I have suggested that stress and panic resulted in two types of group dynamics: one in which the group disintegrated, and one in which the group cohesion increased the conformity of the group. I have described four important episodes of disruption that emerged as the strategic response to the terror event in which the group dynamics framed actions and decisions.

In the military case there were also disruptive events that caused this type of group dynamics. Important events that disrupted the organization were:

First, the decision for Norway's military to participate in the Libyan operation made by the Government on the morning of Friday, 18 March 2011. The politicians and generals were uncoordinated. The commanders of the NJHQ and the NDLO did not seem to be part of the strategic discussions. The Chief of Defence and GIL left their core task and basic principle of broadly discussing Norway's security interests and military strategic objectives before military action was set in motion. Instead, preparations in the tactical organization shaped political and military strategic decisions. This reversal of hierarchical influence was enabled by increased cohesion in 132 LV when the sense of urgency spread in the tactical organization. The group also immediately integrated the local logistics organization even though it belonged to NDLO.

Second, the confirmation made by Prime Minister Stoltenberg on midday on Saturday, 19 March 2011 that Norway would participate with F-16s. This added to the split in the operational hierarchy. Tactics came before operation and led to an extremely fast internal cohesion of 132 LV and a compression of the time horizon to the brink of collapse.

Third, when the site survey team departed to Greece on the afternoon of Sunday, 20 March 2011. The NJHQ was disorganized while 132 LV kept together and handled interactions with the Belgian commander to set the scene for a 24-hour base for the flight operations.

Fourth, when the F-16s deployed to Greece on the morning of Monday, 21 March 2011, 132 LV was speeding up, while NJHQ was still disorganized. The planes had already been diverted from Sicily and landed in Sardinia when they got the message from NJHQ to land in Sicily.

In the military, local tactical groups and networks were mobilized, intertwined with strategic central command during the crisis and dynamic strategic response. The network was enabled by ordinary information and communications technology. Politicians sent text messages to each other informally without mobilizing formal procedures or meetings, such as a government conference, a closed or open meeting with the parliament committee for defence and foreign affairs, or even a meeting of the top military leaders and their advisors. The people who were formally associated with the political and military strategic levels acted as if they were in a tactical operational practice, while the bureaucratic practice and the formal political processes were bypassed.

In the 22 July case, the politicians operated in similar ways. They sent text messages and telephoned people they knew, regardless of their formal positions. The Prime Minister phoned the Deputy National Police Commissioner; the Minister of Justice talked to a local police officer for transport; the Minister's political advisor called just about everyone he thought would provide information, including leaders in the police and the Norwegian Police Security Service; and the Prime Minister's advisor was the source who provided wrong information about the number of causalities to the National Police Commissioner. In reality, there was no functioning hierarchy, but rather a chaotic network of activities, some of which caused more confusion and time loss, and others that contributed to coordination and time gain.

In this disorder, the juridical-bureaucratic practitioners suffered because they were used to procedure and order. They disappeared from the functioning hierarchy, in which according to formalities they supposedly had a role of filling a space between the operational practice and the political practice with strategic advice.

The Formal Levels in the Police Case

Political strategic

1.   Prime Minister
2.   Minister of Justice
3.   Ministry of Justice senior bureaucrats

Police strategic

1.   National Police Commander

Police operational

1.   Deputy National Police Commander
2.   Police Directorate operational staff

Police tactical

1.   District Chief of Police
2.   Deputy Chief of Police (leader of operational staff)
3.   Operational staff
4.   Leader of police district's operations centre
5.   Operations centre operators
6.   Incident commander (coordinator on site)

The Formal Levels in the Military Case

Political strategic

1. Prime Minister
2. Minister of Defence
3. Ministry of Defence senior bureaucrats

Military strategic

1. Chief of Defence
2. Chief of Defence staff/Inspector General of the Air Force
3. Chief of Norwegian Joint Headquarters (NJHQ)

Military operational

1. Defence staff/Operational department
2. Sitsen staff
3. NJHQ staff

Military tactical

1. Commander of 132 LV
2. 132 LV Staff/Commander of the operational planning group

Priorities Confused

The question for both of the studied cases is whether the loss of the bureaucratic strategic element had any effect on the operations. In the police, it did. In the Oslo PD, the senior operational leaders ended up prioritizing the rescue work in the Government complex before and after the events on Utøya came to their attention. Prior to the events on Utøya, they did not prioritize the perpetrator, and later when the first notice of a possible second attack came directly to the Oslo PD operational staff, they did not prioritize cooperation with NBPD or information and decision support to Delta. Meanwhile, Delta acted independently.

The chief of the Oslo PD prioritized the political hierarchy above him (the Government), but bypassed the juridical-bureaucratic leaders in POD even though, according to formal procedure, those leaders were supposed to become operational leaders and to command coordination at the moment when the incident was defined as a national emergency.

In the 22 July case, the contact between the political strategic level and the police strategists was disrupted when the Deputy National Police Commissioner swapped jobs with the National Police Commissioner without informing anyone. The National Police Commissioner was the link to the strategic level through the Crisis Council, where the top bureaucrats working for the Minister of Justice assembled. His deputy was supposed to be the link between the strategic and operational level of the involved police districts (Oslo PD and NBPD).

The deputy's contact with the operational level did not go through the district's chief of police or the district's operational staff leader. Instead, he suddenly took up the role as advisor to the Prime Minister and effectively excluded the National Police Commissioner, who was stuck in POD's operational staff, without any contact with anyone at the strategic level.

As a result, neither the National Police Commissioner nor his deputy communicated clear expectations to the operational-tactical levels. Consequently, the politicians operated as a network, as did the tactical leaders, while there was no particular leadership provided by the people at the operational and strategic levels of the police hierarchy. The operational coordination collapsed.

While the tactical police expected the operational staff and operational centres to coordinate them, the staff and centres became unable to coordinate, resulting in the Delta units having to search in the dark when they arrived near Utøya mainland quay. Delta's practice lies somewhere between the police operational practice and the military operational practice. In the police operational practice, central command and hierarchy is very important. For military operational practitioners, central command is only part of a network.

Delta's immediate pattern of reaction came close to that of a military tactical response. However, this type of reaction did not make any sense to others in the police operational organization, including those in the operations centres and operational networks, who reacted in accordance with normal police operational practice.

In the Libya case, the tactical units acted on behalf of and within their operational structure, although they did not pay much attention to the operational level and the juridical bureaucracy. They thought it was great fun to leave quickly while the bureaucrats still were home for the weekend. The NDLO logistics officer in Bodø thought it was good that he accompanied his 132 LV friends to Greece, even though he belonged to a different organizational unit and his superior said he did not need to go.

In the tactical units, the lack of restrictive order was interpreted to mean that the Government and Chief of Defence intended them to leave at the earliest possible moment. However, if this was the intention then it had no basis in documents, written orders, or formal Government decisions. The whole mobilization for Libya was indeed an expression of pure military operational practice, effectively leaving the juridical-bureaucratic practice without influence.

Leadership and Decision-making in Network Practice

In the military, the idea of network relations and local command had long been discussed with reference to the concepts of network-centric warfare. The military was prepared to use the hierarchy in a flexible way. As the tactical activity speeded up, the most important senior decision was de facto that the strategic leaders needed to stay out of the hierarchical decision-making and just be briefed on the decisions at the tactical level.

The tactical leaders grabbed the initiative and produced the commander's intention, which they then followed. Hence, the commander's intention was an enacted social collaboration that emerged as a result of interactions in the various groups and between many people in the military organization. Locally, in the 132 LV operational planning group, the staff described their experiences of this phenomenon of leadership as belonging to the group, not to a single person.

In contrast, leadership was seen as individual acts in the police. The senior leaders of the police were more inclined to wait for the hierarchy to function. Because the hierarchy collapsed during the operation, there was a serious lack of coordination at crucial boundaries, such as between Oslo PD's operations centre and Kripos, Oslo PD's operational staff and NBPD's operational staff, Delta and Oslo PD's operational staff, and Delta and NBPD's operations centre.

However, there is a difference between the police and the military in that the latter is trained to respond to a crisis within a national command structure, whereas the police handle situations locally within a district, and if needed, ask for help from neighbouring districts. Very rarely will a situation require a national police response like on 22 July 2011. Hence, the national alarm was not prioritized. Police officers, police chiefs, and bureaucrats are not trained to change their response from local to national. Terrorism is probably the only emergency situation that would generate anything close to a national police response. Even if national emergency is a rare scenario, it should not have been outside the police preparations.

Although the military organization operated within a relatively clear national command structure, people to a large degree acted outside this structure. As a result, many leaders were genuinely surprised by the speed of the mobilization.

It is a paradox that the police force, trained as it were to act locally, was delayed because the force did not coordinate in accordance with pre-planned national structures, while the military speeded up because it broke its national structure and acted locally.

In the Libya case, contact was evidently good between the political and strategic levels, at least between the Minister of Defence and the Chief of Defence. The Prime Minister's role in the strategic discussions is unclear. There is nothing to suggest that the Chief of Defence challenged the strategic decision to deploy Norwegian forces to fight against Gaddafi in Libya.

It was Sitsen that handled much of the operational preparations and directly briefed the Chief of Defence and Minister of Defence. However, those leaders did not interfere in the operational preparations and coordination. The most important network decisions were reportedly made in discussions between Sitsen, GIL, and the operations planning group at 132

LV. However, the Chief of Defence and the Minister of Defence did not recognize the need for coherent strategic leadership or any structured strategic process that would help them make strategic judgements in the event.

In the Ministry of Defence, Sitsen functioned as a hub for coordination and surveillance of information between tactical and strategic decision-makers. In this sense, it took the NJHQ's role in the preparation phase, when time was of the essence.

Emergent Network Strategies

Coordination of information collapsed in the police on 22 July, due to confusion between the roles of the various strategic, operational, and tactical leaders in the Ministry of Justice, POD, and the two police districts (Oslo PD and NBPD). The collapse originated in confusion regarding the coordination of roles. POD is the operational coordinator in national emergencies, while the local police district's operational staff is the coordinator in local emergencies. As the events of 22 July 2011 constituted both a local and national emergency, confusion arose between the various levels in the hierarchy.

Oslo PD's chief of police was never in contact with his superiors in POD, but he wanted better communication between himself and the Prime Minister. However, to use tactical and operational leaders to inform the Prime Minister in a phase when everything was chaotic might have contributed to unnecessary overstretching of the resources and might have influenced the operational leadership collapse. Attention and resources were drawn away from the operational response. A leadership vacuum emerged at the core of the operation when operational leaders were fleeing upwards in the hierarchy to support the Prime Minister.

In his public statements, Prime Minister Stoltenberg contributed to the confusion when he claimed not to have interfered in the operational work. However, he had demanded continuous updates on the operational work from a number of the operational leaders after not receiving any news from the 'strategic level'.

In the Libya case, the operational strategy emerged during the preparations. Libya had not been part of anyone's strategy in the weeks and days before the UN's decision, and the need to put previous plans aside and to improvise was recognized at all levels in the hierarchy. Even when the operation officially became a NATO operation some days later, the NATO commander did not have a strategy in the form of a plan or objective.

The Inspector General of the Air Force (GIL) discussed directly with 132 LV without linking the NJHQ to the strategic and tactical level. He contacted and was briefed by the major in charge of the operations planning group. The operational level with the Commander of the NJHQ was not given responsibility for the planning of the mission during the first weekend of mobilization. This short-circuiting was the main cause of the breakdown in the normal strategic/operational/tactical hierarchy, leading to time gain during the preparations for deployment. However, it also resulted in the emergence of a strategy dealing with the past, not the future.

When the Delta units accelerated out of Oslo PD towards Utøya, they were not under any active tactical or operational control or guidance by Oslo PD or NBPD. According to the 22 July Commission's report, the Delta units acted first and informed their superiors later, thus contributing to the patterns of action being formed before the plan, i.e. strategy was made sense of as past behaviour.

Hence, both of the specialized groups Delta and 132 LV were instrumental in shaping the operational strategies in the *present* and as sensemaking *after* the actions rather than as plans *before* the actions. What enabled this in the formal hierarchies of both the police and the military was a major cut-off or collapse at the operational level, between the strategic and tactical levels.

Reference

Uppsala Conflict Data Program (2016). Department of Peace and Conflict Research. http://ucdp.uu.se/#country/620, retrieved October 2016.

14 Conclusions

A Complexity Approach to the Study of Emergency and Crisis

Since the 1990s a growing body of literature has emerged within the field of organizational complexity research (see an overview in Johannessen & Kuhn, 2012, Volume I-IV). When researchers in the 1990s were to describe organizational dynamics in the emerging age of globalization and rapid change, organizations were being referred to as operating on the 'edge of chaos' (Pascale, Millemann & Gioja, 2000). Since the turn of the millennium, however, advanced social theory has been brought into contact with complexity research to form a new understanding of dynamic organizing as complex responsive processes and practice (Stacey, 2010).

The present study takes into account these developments in theory to enquire into two cases of emergency and crisis-handling organizations (i.e. the police and the military) that operate between two very distinct patterns of action: a 'slow' mode when hierarchical organization dominates, and a 'fast' mode that emerges during emergencies and crises, in which hierarchical organization changes or even falls apart into a form of network organizing.

This study is an attempt to understand the details of complex organizational processes in dramatic situations. Far from being exhaustive, the study offers a potential new perspective on what complexity means in terms of practice in organizations during emergencies and crises. This perspective implies increased awareness of the way processes of communication, identity, power, and ethics emerge as practice.

A key argument of this book is that the aforementioned processes are understood and made sense of very differently in bureaucratic and operational practices, which makes it difficult to coordinate a common practice and a common sense during emergency and crisis.

Awareness of Communication: Organization

Communication is at the centre of organizing, in the sense that communicating is not only an activity that takes place in organizations, but also the processes by which human organizing is constructed (Taylor & Van Every, 2000). In many operational groups, there is an idea that when everything is calm and stable (i.e. in peacetime), discussion is allowed, whereas during an emergency or a crisis there must be strict hierarchy and no discussion.

Clearly, the kind of discussion or conversation that people could engage in when not in an emergency is different from the kind of discussion or conversation they could engage in when they are in an emergency or crisis operation. However, no emergency or crisis is hectic all of the time: there are different calm and hectic times and spaces in which the quality of communication practices are crucial.

Calm and Hectic Spaces

The precise giving of short messages or orders, which is often considered the best way when time is running out, is not necessarily the best way if a group is not capable of handling the short messages because of stress, panic, or other phenomena; short messages can be misunderstood or understood very differently.

Talking during calm periods can pull members of a group together, increase the group's preparedness and rational thought, and reduce stress both immediately and when the time horizon shrinks and the hectic period is on again. To use the *calm spaces* to make sense could be advantageous in the *hectic spaces*.

In the 22 July case, there was a period of 30 minutes while Delta officers were in their cars on their way to Utøya. For the two P30 officers, there were 14 minutes when they were in their car before they reached Utøya mainland quay, and five minutes when they were hiding behind a container. Those intervals provided space for talk. What kind of talk would have been useful?

Talk

It would not only have been useful with operational and tactical talk, but also with talk intended to appeal to feelings and morale, to reduce stress, and to boost a sense of togetherness and responsibility for each other in the face of danger.

Research has highlighted the importance of communication by talking when dealing with stressful situations (Sutton & Kahn, 1987). It is no coincidence that communication by talking is one of the characteristics of operational practices, in contrast to bureaucratic practices. Sharing of information and acknowledgement of the function of information to hold loosely coupled informal networks in coordination are integrated into these practices. The amount of talking is associated with reliable performance (Weick, 2001, p. 143).

Talking before a situation emerges has its advantages. After 22 July 2011, senior leaders in the Oslo PD complained that the communication between different units before that day had not been the best. During the emergency, much of the talking was infused with distrust and characterized by lack of previous contact between police districts and within the hierarchy.

On 22 July, the amount of talking could have been reduced for some of the politicians who became hyperactive. However, many others, particularly the operational leaders, talked too little and not with the right people during the emergency. They did not manage to direct their talk so that it would help them find the right timing between the amount of talking and the time horizon. The issue was not only one of the amount, direction, and timing of the talking, but also of the quality.

In the military, the amount of talking seemed well balanced in terms of these aspects, at least for some groups. People knew and trusted each other across hierarchical levels, and therefore the talking continued to be constructive during the whole phase of preparations for deployment. The exceptions were the generals, who failed to raise important issues about strategy with the politicians, and the NJHQ and 132 LV, who communicated too little about operational and tactical coordination and responsibilities.

Disruptions of Communication and the Effects on Stress and Panic

There was stress and panic in both the police and the military organizations. In the 22 July case, there were many moments that disrupted the organization, but there were four serious situations that led to immediate consequences for the speed of the police operation, as well as long-term consequences in terms of massive public critique of the organization.

The first moment occurred when the senior leaders of the Oslo PD, the Police Directorate, and the Ministry of Justice acted in response to the bomb in Oslo. The second disruptive moment happened when NBPD responded to the shootings on Utøya. The third moment was the decision to change the rally point from Utøya mainland quay to Storøya, 3.6 km away from the shortest crossing to Utøya, and the fourth important moment of organizational disruption happened when the Delta units overloaded the boats that were to take them to Utøya.

In the Libya case, I also focused on four disruptive situations that had major effects on the trajectory of events: the UN's decision of a no-fly zone to protect civilians in Libya, Prime Minister Stoltenberg's public declaration of Norway's participation, the speedy departure of an Air Force site survey team to Greece, and the first F-16 deployment on the following day.

These disruptive situations demonstrated a link between stress and the trade-off between tightening and splitting of groups. This was seen in many groups at all levels of the hierarchy in both the police and the military. However, the dynamics had different outcomes; group cohesion was an asset in some situations and a drawback in others. A collapse of hierarchical levels was beneficial in some situations, because important parts of the organization could operate as a network and speed up interactions. In other situations, however, the organization disintegrated into chaotic interactions, leading to loss of valuable time.

Delta had a problem associated with their tightly coupled group. When relatively small errors occurred, the effects rippled through the whole group and affected the group's functionality. This occurred in the communication between a Delta member and the operations centre about the rally point, in the actual decision to change the rally point, and when the boat was over-loaded. The positive side of the tightly coupled group was that the levels of stress diminished.

In the 22 July case, the organizational response was highly complex and fragmented, with different groups responding in an uncoordinated manner at the same time. Delta's overloading of the boat can be seen as a lack of necessary flexibility and subgrouping. At the same time, we saw how the P30 splitting of work tasks increased flexibility, but produced paralysis.

By contrast, Delta's cohesion enabled its units to mobilize their moral strength to face the fear, physical hardship, and problems of information deficit—the cluster that von Clausewitz termed the *friction of war* (Kiesling, 2001). With manageable stress levels, the Delta units could confront a very uncertain and potentially deadly situation. They encountered a terrorist with wires visible on his body, but they managed to judge them as harmless mobile phone cables. No shots were fired and the terrorist surrendered and was arrested, which meant he could be brought to trial. This might not have happened if Delta's stress levels had been too high.

Hierarchy and Knowledge

Pluralistic ignorance (Miller & McFarland, 1987) means that people as-sume those with more seniority, higher rank, and more experience under-stand or know more about a situation than others, so there is no reason to question or discuss what is going on. We saw this phenomenon when NBPD abandoned its responsibility to decide the rally point because it thought Delta was more suited to make the decision. It turned out Delta did not have a clue about where to establish the rally point.

There were similar tendencies in the Libya case, as people at the tactical level expressed that even if they did not know why they were in a hurry, they were sure that the generals were aware of the bigger picture. This demon-strated eloquently how the military constructed a reality on upon which it acted. No one could clearly say why they sped up the mobilization or broke the rules, practices, and well established procedures. Instead of questioning the speedy and fuzzy political decision, the military accepted and reiterated the explanation given by the politicians about the Libyan population being on the brink of mass murder by Gaddafi's forces.

The tactical levels of the military organization assumed the higher ranks knew what they were doing and that those 'at the top' had a strategy that the tactical level was about to implement. They settled with the thought that someone at the top of the hierarchy had decided the need for urgency and that 'someone' had control of the operation. Basically, the military did what they were trained to do, though not only clearly based on orders, but also on their own assumptions of what lack of orders meant. The absence of orders to hold back was interpreted to mean they should speed up. The logic of pluralistic ignorance was therefore released into a very dangerous international situation.

Related to the interpersonal communication failure of pluralistic ignorance is the phenomenon of false hypothesis. In the military, a false hypothesis evolved in terms of the factual scale and risk of Gaddafi's attacks on civilians in Libya. The lack of structure around the strategic analysis of the situation left the hypothesis unquestioned. In the 22 July case, Delta hypothesized that there were three to five terrorists. This influenced the change in the rally point and the subsequent time loss. When Delta years later publically tried to explain the overloaded rubber boat, they still reiterated the false hypothesis of three to five terrorists as an explanation for their actions.

Awareness of Power: Hierarchy and Authority

Hierarchies are attempts to clarify and order responsibility and power relations in one dimension or direction, from the top down. However, in a crisis, operational organizations' responsibility and power relations emerge between people in many directions and dimensions. Phenomena that are associated with hierarchy, such as power, leadership, and change, emerge in the interaction between people and spread across local structures in the organization. Since this for the individual actor creates a lack of overview and undermines the formal hierarchy, those who manage the hierarchy – top leaders – will become eager to limit the employees' activity to that which is controllable within the hierarchy.

Within POD, the Ministry of Justice, and the Government, hierarchical constraints were imposed on communication, and led to centralization of communication. A press conference with the police was cancelled because the Prime Minister wanted to inform the public first. The need for centralized control led to total confusion around the number of casualties when the police, instead of independently checking the numbers, trusted and released the wrong numbers they received from the Prime Minister's office.

Stress did not increase the salience of formal structure and authority relations in the Libya case, but in the 22 July case there were clear indications of this, at least for strategic and operational leaders. They seemed eager to re-establish formal hierarchy and authority but ended up abandoning the operational level. In the interaction between Delta and NBPD, the expert hierarchy increased its salience while the formal structure collapsed.

Collapse of the Operational Level

In both organizations, the most significant collapse of the formal organization happened at the operational level. In the military, the operational level collapsed functionally, but it operated as expected in terms of time and speed. In the police, the operational level collapsed both functionally and in terms of time and speed.

Worth noting, however, is the way that people at the strategic and tactical levels of the military organization rapidly started to coordinate without involving those at the operational level. Part of the explanation for this top- and bottom-level cohesion and middle-level exclusion could be that leaders who were assigned to the strategic and tactical levels were situated in close proximity in or around Oslo, including those in the information coordination hub, Sitsen. The operational headquarters (NJHQ) are situated a 1000 km from Oslo and people there were physically disconnected from the community of decision-makers in Oslo. The NJHQ is set up for longer-term planning and command of operations, not for crisis. The strategic leaders in Oslo seemed to be aware of this as they bypassed the NJHQ and allowed the tactical practitioners to do the same.

In the early phase of the 22 July emergency, Oslo PD did not pay much attention to POD. As the Utøya incident emerged, Oslo PD and NBPD rapidly needed operational coordination, yet that never happened because both police districts were occupied with the incident in their own districts. The link between them was Delta, but no one coordinated Delta as the unit rushed from Oslo PD into the NBPD's area.

The Transition from Hierarchy to Network

In the studied cases, the military handled the transition from hierarchical to non-hierarchical organization well in terms of time, speed, and tactical considerations, while the police did not. However, in light of political and strategic criteria, the military did not function well because they did not hold back to give themselves time to assess the crisis in political and strategic terms.

In the police, as events unfolded, the political and strategic levels failed to function with necessary distance from the tactical level. The leaders in the hierarchy 'above' the operational leaders distracted them from coordinating the police operation. Both network dynamics and hierarchical dynamics operated in parallel and were intertwined. However, the organization and leaders did not seem prepared and coordinated for the shift in dynamics and what that would mean and require in terms of group actions and leadership. The emerging network dynamics seemed to happen randomly.

Improvisation

Improvisation might reduce the impact of a crisis, but improvisation is difficult when stress levels are high and role patterns are strict (Stein, 2004). On 22 July, many police officers of all ranks were not pre-trained in the roles they took or were expected to take during the emergency. In the parts of the operation that were successful, such as the immediate organizing on the ground after the bomb blast, many actors later expressed that it was a matter of luck that some of the most experienced tactical officers were on duty and available on that particular afternoon.

In other parts of the operation, the lack of pre-training had large consequences. However, it is surprising that very experienced leaders in POD abandoned their roles and formal responsibility. When interactions and networks became very loose and developed into a form for which the operational, strategic, and political practitioners were unprepared, they collapsed in concert with the organization.

In the military, roles and responsibilities were highly pre-trained and tight at the tactical level. The tightness of the organization made the roles vulnerable to collapse due to errors. To succeed they became dependent on chance. Situations such as the borrowing of a Hercules plane, the availability of people to make a functional Operation Planning Group at 132 LV, the phone call that made Sitsen aware that the site survey team could travel with a Belgian transport plane to Greece, and many other situations were all lucky coincidences that enabled the organization to function in haste without serious mistakes.

The Importance of Knowing and Trusting Each Other

Although both the police and the military often change teams and working relations, the importance of this change in the studied cases was diverse. In the police, there were many incidences of people who did not speak up or attempt to clarify. The patterns seemed to reflect a dysfunctional power culture. Difficulties with coordination rooted in this power culture occurred within POD, within Oslo PD, between POD and the police districts, and between Delta and NBPD's operations centre. Many of the people in these groups and organizations were more concerned with their own position than with solving the problems at hand.

The consequences of this were clearly visible in the case of Oslo PD, where the power issues made them incompetent in stopping the terrorist from escaping. The operations centre and its leader were bypassed by the operational staff and the incident commander, while at the same time the operations centre ignored a message delivered by a civilian phone service operator, an 'outsider'. The message contained information that was enough to stop the terrorist had it been acted upon.

In the military, the response was restricted to the Air Force and the logistics support from the NDLO. Many of the key persons who were involved knew and trusted each other from before. The exception was the interaction between 132 LV and the NJHQ. It was bureaucratic in style. Perhaps this was due to the fact that the NJHQ had not participated in a major exercise that had been carried out just weeks earlier, where they could have rehearsed the particular operational-tactical team relations between the units.

The cases demonstrate the need to pay attention to power issues and interpersonal skills during emergency and crisis. These skills can be selected, trained, and developed. In the RNoAF, people are highly selected, trained, and developed as officers and specialists. They know each other, and know who to call and to trust. During the crisis, this made the organization more likely to succeed than the police, in which the power issues and levels of interpersonal skills varied considerably.

Awareness of Identity: Strategy

Emergent Strategies in the Cases

The results of the study challenge the traditional idea of strategic planning of future action. In the cases, strategies and operational activities rather emerged as a dynamic paradox when the actors engaged in planning and acting for the immediate future while at the same time they tried to make sense of the emerging situation in light of the immediate past. This alludes to a circular understanding of time, and hence strategy, rather than a sequential one.

In the Libya case, when the mobilization gained momentum, it produced compression of the time horizon. Strategies in the form of planning lagged behind and in reality the organization dealt with the past. In order to adapt what had already happened to the strategies that were supposed to be about the future, the actors had to expand their time horizon by, for example, issuing orders three weeks after the orders had already been carried out.

The RNoAF's mobilization for war in Libya revealed that coordinated patterns of action do not need an overall plan, shared understanding, visions, total overviews, and unified cultures. Rather, the quality and dynamics of communication patterns, power relations, and the experience of identity and ethics within and between groups were decisive for how widespread and coordinated organizational patterns of action emerged. In practical terms, these qualities enabled persons to act with great flexibility by following procedures, putting aside procedures, and taking both expected and unexpected initiatives in a deployment to a completely unknown region where they had no idea what they would encounter.

The Question of Time in the Military

In contrast to strategy in a traditional sense (i.e. as an overarching, clear plan for the future), the strategies in the studied cases emerged not as rational hierarchical decision-making in a linear time horizon, but as *sensemaking in a complex, stretched-out time horizon*.

For some of the tactical units, the time horizon slowed down in response to confusion, and strategies then became compressed in time. Strategies are meaningful patterns of action and when these became compressed in time, the construction of meaning (sensemaking) happened within a shorter time horizon than normal strategic decision-making.

In both studied cases, responding strategies emerged earlier than the normal time horizon within which they were supposed to happen. The official strategies that should be formulated by people at the organization's strategic level thus became *intentions about the past*. The difference between the military and the police was that in the military the fast strategy of the 132 LV did not encounter major coordination problems, while in the police, the fast strategy of Delta did encounter coordination problems.

The Libya case demonstrated that strategies emerged very quickly in a situation of crisis. Not only did this happen on a local scale at 132 LV, but it also happened on a large international and global scale, when many countries separately and as part of multinational institutions and coalitions rapidly launched military operations without any form of strategy in the orthodox sense. The strategies were shaped both during the course of event and after the event.

The Question of Time in the Police

In the 22 July case, many professional individuals and groups, in addition to volunteers, responded spontaneously. However, the tendency for the police groups was not consistent. Some clung to the hierarchy, some disregarded their hierarchical responsibilities, and others were task-oriented without any idea that coordination with others was needed. The organization fell apart, but in the subsequent chaos the organization and various groups did not become entirely dysfunctional because the operation *did* approach Utøya and the terrorist was arrested.

However, when people are systematically executed on an island within a relatively short time horizon, questions must be asked whether some of those minutes and people could have been saved. Public expectations of emergency response professionalism often amount to little or no tolerance for errors by those who are responsible for responding to acts of terrorism. Public inquiries following such events often focus on how rules and regulations have been met during the crisis or emergency response. The inquiries will inevitably find that formalities were broken and consequently they will level criticism. 22 July 2011 was no exception.

However, the 22 July Commission failed to explore, explain, and tell the story of organizational complexity in the police operation. This story is one of disrupted hierarchy, stress, panic, groupthink, lack of leadership, and other phenomena that rippled through the organization and caused the formal response patterns to collapse into fragmented groups and individuals operating without any organizational coordination.

This is not only a story of individual actions, judgements, and decisions in a complex emergency operation, but also of how such individual actions were enabled, constrained, and paralyzed by the breakdown of hierarchies and emergence of network organizing constructed by patterns of communication, power, identity, and ethics.

The Questions of Time Taken Together

In the military, the people at the political and professional strategic level of the hierarchy acted in a time-compressed network (gaining time) and the operational hierarchy acted in a time-expanded hierarchy (losing time). The hierarchy and time horizon stretched to organizational collapse, resulting in the loss of coordination and diminished opportunity for sensemaking and quality in decision-making. Between, but hierarchically below, the strategic and operational levels, the tactical level was trained to operate as a network. Those at the tactical level rocketed into time-compressed network organizing, and passed between the strategic level's time-compressed horizon and operational level's time-expanded horizon. The tactical functioning was good; the problem was lack of coordination with the operational level.

In the 22 July case, the Prime Minister bypassed the professional strategic level and approached the operational level to save time. However, this was unsuccessful, because the people at the operational level had lost coordination with the fast-moving tactical practitioners, who operated on their own.

The tactical response from Delta and the NBPD were too uncoordinated to function properly, due to their different time horizons. Delta speeded up as the NBPD slowed down. When the two tactical units came into contact and needed coordination, confusion emerged. Delta then rushed off and fortunately met another NBPD tactical unit with a boat. The operational centres of the police had no idea of what was going on in these encounters.

In the military, the response was down to the RNoAF, which coordinated at the tactical level. Quite remarkable network coordination occurred between the tactical unit 132 LV and the local logistics unit, the NDLO. Since the units belonged to two different command structures, it was not given that their interaction should maintain the necessary speed, but it did. This together with the coordinating efforts of Sitsen, the lack of strategic analysis to slow them down, and the decoupling of the NJHQ were crucial factors for the emergence of the fast strategy.

Awareness of Ethics: Leadership

Small Scale and Large Scale

I started out in the introduction chapter by saying that the purpose of this study has been to describe and interpret the organizational complexity and dynamics in two cases of emergency and crisis, with a particular view towards how strategies and leadership emerge in situations that are out of the ordinary.

The two cases verify that organizations that respond to emergencies and crises are most volatile in tensions between small-scale and large-scale actions and effects. In the Libya case, the crucial criterion for success was the small-scale RNoAF's response to a large-scale international crisis. In the 22 July case, the criterion for success was the large-scale cross-organizational response to two specific episodes of terror. The events had a large-scale destructive impact, but they were small-scale in terms of being confined to a small geographical area and in terms of being acted out by a single terrorist.

In both cases, interruptions were stressful and made a great impact on both disintegration and the cohesion of groups. However, the military seemed more trained to deal with the type of activity it was preparing (an international operation), but it was stressed by the tempo of the fighter pilot unit 132 LV. The quality of leadership was higher in the military than in the police, which seemed more dependent on acting according to plans. When no one followed the plans, the police response repertoire narrowed because the police had no experience of responding to a terrorist act, let alone two different types of attacks in two different locations in two different police districts.

Political and Professional Leadership

In the political sensemaking process following the dramatic events of the two cases, strategies were portrayed as pre-planned, rational, and controlled. In the Libya case, this form of constructed rationality took place as part of the process of establishing the historical truth, when political actors used all of their skills to defend and portray events as being entirely in the legitimate interests of the international community, participating countries, and the people of Libya, while the personal motives and interests of politicians were kept firmly in the dark.

For instance, the House of Commons' report demonstrated how the Libya intervention was largely about the personal interests of Prime Minister David Cameron in the UK and President Nicolas Sarkozy in France. Such personal interests would also have been an important factor for Prime Minister Jens Stoltenberg in Norway. There is no evidence to suggest that he was interested in checking facts with experts, hearing counterarguments, or discussing them publically with the Norwegian parliament (Stortinget), as would have been the wise thing to do. Clearly, he was interested in showing his loyalty to the great allied powers, the UK, France, and the USA, even though the USA was more reluctant in the early phase. Regardless, three years later Stoltenberg was appointed Secretary General of NATO.

In the intertwining of political ethics and personal interests with unclear links to any national interests, a serious question must also be raised about the professional ethics of the generals. By not insisting on forging a political and military strategy before deployment, they failed in their professional role, which was to underpin any decisions about military action with deeper strategic and political analyses. They left their strategies to the fate of emerging events.

In this respect, the Chief of Defence and his generals failed to see the operational risks associated with the compression of the time horizon. As a consequence of this misplaced loyalty, the generals also failed in their moral obligation to understand the role of the military in a democracy. It seemed war had become normalized to the degree that no one objected even in the clear absence of strategy.

In reality, although loosely sanctioned by the UN, the politicians and the generals jointly embarked on a military attack on another country without discussing strategy or demanding a broader discussion of what national and international interests they were protecting by bombing Gaddafi's forces and legitimizing the assassination of the state leader Gaddafi.

The End of Command and Control: Leadership as Common Sense and Different Sense

Common sense and leadership are interrelated. During a crisis or an emergency, especially smaller groups can become so consumed and blinded by their cohesion that the group members refuse to be functional even when the tasks ahead call for flexibility. Unless they are brought out of their cohesive mode to reflect on the emerging paradox of the common and different sense of the group, the group will be at risk of becoming dysfunctional. Resulting from stress and panic, extreme group cohesion (groupthink) and extreme fragmentation (total splitting) can emerge rapidly during an emergency or crisis. The studied cases support and expand that a leader will have to interfere in emerging organizational patterns, whether the pattern is one of too much fragmentation or too much cohesion. This interference is not one of command and control. The leader's challenge is one of talking, timing, direction, and quality.

The findings of this study imply that leaders in crisis and emergency operations need a highly complex view of hierarchy, central command, control, and support, taking into account that hierarchy has time dimensions that vertically and horizontally distort the normal hierarchical time horizon for practices at different levels.

Crisis and emergency operations always evolve within a time horizon. Ideally, the response should follow the normal time horizon. *Emergencies* often require extremely time-compressed responses from the tactical units, because the situation requires a response within a time horizon of minutes or up to hours at the most. This requires a reversed hierarchy.

In a *crisis*, the time horizon is from several hours up to several days, weeks, and months. The need for time compression is low within the normal time horizon of the organizational practices and formal levels. The ordinary hierarchy can function with strategic, operational, and tactical levels involved and intact.

In the 22 July emergencies, there was a need for reversed hierarchical functioning, but with operational coordination. While the tactical level did respond, it was not coordinated. There were different time horizons within the tactical level that ultimately caused confusion. At the same time, the operational coordination was rendered impossible because operational leaders drifted 'upwards' in the hierarchy to satisfy the strategic and political level, 'ripping' apart the operational coordination of the organization.

In the Libya crisis, the hierarchy was also reversed, but it was needless and reckless, because it ended with the abdication of strategic and operational leadership, the compromising of strategy, and the production of a false hypothesis at the tactical level, which in turn fed into the eagerness to drop bombs in a way that shaped and changed the strategic and operational objectives.

In both cases, the one that lost time and the one that gained time, the time horizons changed because of lack of leadership. In the police, they lost time because they were too fragmented. They needed leadership to coordinate them and become more cohesive. In the military, they gained time because they were too cohesive. They needed leadership to break up and slow down the speed of the organization. That is perhaps the most surprising finding of this study.

When organizational processes escalate, leaders have important roles in slowing down the speed of events, just as they can contribute to speed up whenever organizational processes stagnate or move slowly. However, their actions involve risk. Leaders can only slow down or speed up processes into which they are coupled. Their actions intervene in the causes of further actions and responses, and might construct consequences of which the leaders have no control.

The social phenomena of trust and authority are of vital importance in groups and organizations during crisis and emergency operations. Groups with *low* levels of trust and weak authority relations will likely be vulnerable to fragmentation. Groups with *high* levels of trust and strong authority relations will likely be cohesive and vulnerable to lack of creative and critical thinking.

The role of the crisis and emergency leader is to both support and counter the dynamics of these phenomena by constantly directing gestures of *cohesion and fragmentation* into the group/organization in order to maintain the paradoxical dynamics needed for the group/organization to deal with the complexities of crisis and emergency operations.

References

Johannessen, S. O. & Kuhn, L. (eds) (2012). *Complexity in Organization Studies, Volume I–IV*. London: Sage.

Kiesling, E. C. (2001). On war without the fog. *Military Review*, September–October, pp. 85–87.

Miller, D. T. & McFarland, C. (1987). Pluralistic ignorance: When similarity is interpreted as dissimilarity. *Journal of Personality and Social Psychology*, 53, pp. 298–305.

Pascale, R. T., Millemann, M. & Gioja, L. (2000). *Surfing the Edge of Chaos: The Laws of Nature and the New Laws of Business*. New York: Crown Business.

Stacey, R. D. (2010). *Complexity and Organizational Reality*. London: Routledge.

Stein, M. (2004). The critical period of disasters: Insights from sensemaking and psychoanalytic theory. *Human Relations*, 57(10), pp. 1243–1261.

Sutton, R. I. & Kahn, R. L. (1987). Prediction, understanding, and control as antidotes to organizational stress. In: J. W. Lorch (ed.). *Handbook of Organizational Behaviour*. Englewood Cliffs, NJ: Prentice Hall, pp. 272–285.

Taylor, J. R. & Van Every, E. J. (2000). *The Emergent Organization: Communication as Its Site and Surface*. Mahwah, NJ: Lawrence Erlbaum.

Weick, K. E. (2001). *Making Sense of Organization*. Malden, MA: Blackwell.

Appendix 1
Map of Oslo and Utøya

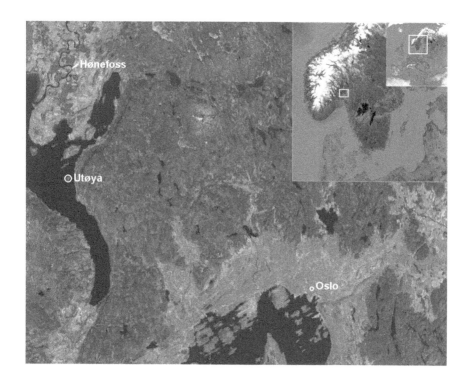

Appendix 2
Map of Utøya area

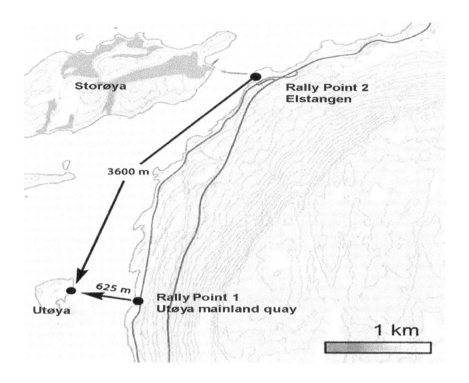

Index